Eating for
Sustained
Energy 3

Liesbet Delport RD(SA) and Gabi Steenkamp RD(SA)

Dedication

To all those with diabetes, who for so long have had to eat foods containing no sugar and often tasting like cardboard. Thanks to the glycemic index, they can now savour lower fat, lower GI foods that are best for anyone who wishes to enjoy sustained energy.

Acknowledgements

A great big thank you to our families for their patience and support while we prepared and tried out all these dishes, until they were perfect.

A word of thanks to Liesbet's daughters Aurelia and Leaan for submitting several recipes, and setting out the initial recipe analysis.

Thank you also to John who contributed recipes to this book.

Thank you to Daniella, Gabi's trusted assistant, for her patience and the long hours spent assisting in carefully proofreading all the manuscripts.

Thank you to Neville and Susan for the excellent photography and styling of the dishes in this book.

Thank you to all our colleagues for your support and enthusiastic use of all our books among your patients.

Last, but not least, our thanks to the publisher, Ansie Kamffer, and the editor, Danya Ristić, for their faith in this project.

We also humbly acknowledge the hand of the Lord in bringing this book to fruition.

First published in 2008

Tafelberg

Tafelberg, an imprint of NB Publishers
40 Heerengracht, Cape Town, 8000

First edition, first impression 2008

Copyright © published edition: Tafelberg (2008)
Copyright © text: Liesbet Delport and Gabi Steenkamp (2008)

Publisher Ansie Kamffer
Editor Danya Ristić
Proofreader Roxanne Reid
Photography Neville Lockhart
Food stylist Susan Bosman
Typesetting Gerhardt van Rooyen
Printed and bound by WKT Company Limited, China

ISBN-10: 0-624-04615-X
ISBN-13: 978-0-624-0461-8

Disclaimer
Although the authors and publisher have made every effort to ensure that the information in this book was accurate at the time of going to press, they accept no responsibility for any loss, injury or inconvenience sustained by any person using this book or following the advice in it.

Contents

Authors' Foreword

When we compiled *Eating for Sustained Energy*, we had seven aims: we wanted each recipe to be tasty, quick and easy to make, using ingredients that are affordable and readily available in any home, while also being lower in fat and having a lower glycemic index (GI) than traditional recipes. Our readers assure us regularly that we have achieved each and every one of these aims.

In fact, we have had so many requests from satisfied readers for more recipes that we compiled *Eating for Sustained Energy 2* and revamped *Eating for Sustained Energy 1*. The original was written eight years ago, and so the nutrition information needed to be brought in line with the latest research. The revamped version has all the new glycemic load (GL) information, as well as the latest GI values of foods tested over the last seven years.

In response to the many requests for more lower GI, lower fat recipes, we decided to put together this book, *Eating for Sustained Energy 3*. The recipes comply with all our original aims, but we have also used many new modern flavour fusions, while keeping them quick and easy to prepare.

When we started writing *Eating for Sustained Energy*, we had no publisher and we had no idea that recipes of this type would be so popular. What we did have was lots of enthusiasm and the knowledge that it is not that difficult to compile tasty, healthy recipes. In fact, we were both cooking and baking such dishes for our families every day! And we felt they should be shared with you, the public.

Now, after eight years, we know that these recipes work! Used regularly, they help to lower blood glucose levels of those with diabetes, and to reduce cholesterol levels, blood pressure, hyperinsulinemia and insulin resistance, as well as to alleviate the symptoms of chronic candida, polycystic ovarian syndrome (PCOS) and inflammatory diseases such as arthritis. They also help children who suffer from Attention Deficit (Hyperactivity) Disorder to concentrate, overweight people to lose weight more easily, fatigued people to have more energy, and sportsmen and -women to perform better.

As previously, we have included the GL value in the nutritional boxes. This is explained, in easy-to-understand terms, in the Introduction. Unlike the GI, you can add up the GL values of all your meals and snacks and get your total GL per day.

Our handy *South African Glycemic Index and Load Guide* has also proved to be of great help to many. It helps you quickly and easily to find the GI and GL of most carbohydrate-containing foods eaten in South Africa, as it includes a cross-referenced alphabetical list of foods. Fat, fibre, protein, carbohydrate and kJ content per typical portion of food are also listed. Many people like to keep the *Guide* with them when they shop, so that they can easily check the GI of any food. This guide has been updated once again in 2007, and also has a partner in the form of the *South African Fat and Protein Guide*, which contains information about different types of fats and proteins in typical South African foods.

Our book on weight management, *Eat Smart and Stay Slim: The GI Diet*, also contains a few recipes and a handy section on "meals for a week", which allows you to combine any breakfast, lunch, dinner and two to three snacks per day and still lose weight. Other information on how to get off the treadmill of compulsive eating, on label-reading skills and fat-proofing your meals, as well as motivation to start exercising, is also included.

Eat Smart for Sport guides the professional and amateur sportsperson, and concerned parents, on exactly what and how much should be consumed before, during and after training and competition, as well as how to use the GI and GL to gain the competitive edge.

Our recipe books *Eating for Sustained Energy 1, 2* and *3*, as well *Sustained Energy for Kids* and *Snacks and Treats for Sustained Energy 1*, give you many more delicious recipes to help with weight management, blood glucose control, general healthy eating and improved sports performance.

May you enjoy this book as much as all the others.

Introduction

Most people feel they could do with more sustained energy. Feeling tired or chronically exhausted and having no energy seems to be the norm in our modern, stressed world. We believe that most of the solution lies in eating correctly.

The glycemic index (GI)

By learning how to use the glycemic index (GI) and consuming a lower fat diet, we can attain a sustained supply of energy. Resorting to all sorts of "pick-me-up-quick" tonics or caffeine, alcohol or cigarettes to relax, will no longer be necessary. Carbohydrate is the body's main source of fuel and consuming the right type and amount at the proper time should ensure sustained energy, instead of you feeling hyped up one moment and flat the next. Eating the lower fat way and following the GI will regulate blood glucose levels, keeping them stable, and will result in feeling great all the time.

In the past, it was assumed that complex carbohydrates or starches, such as potatoes, mealie-meal and bread, were digested and absorbed slowly, resulting in only a slight rise in blood glucose levels. Simple sugars, by contrast, were believed to be digested and absorbed quickly, producing a large and rapid rise in blood glucose levels. We now know that these assumptions are incorrect, and that the general public, as well as people with diabetes, no longer need to avoid sugar altogether, provided they use it correctly. In fact, we now know that table sugar has a slightly more favourable effect on blood glucose levels than do potatoes, bread and a few other starches if used on their own.

As early as the 1930s, scientists challenged the assumption that "all carbohydrates are created equal" and that the metabolic effects of carbohydrates can be predicted by classifying them as either "simple" or "complex". In the 1970s, researchers such as Otto and Crapo examined the glycemic impact of a range of foods containing carbohydrate. To standardise the interpretation of glycemic response data, that is, the effect of food on blood glucose levels, Jenkins and colleagues of the University of Toronto, Canada, proposed the GI in 1981.

The glycemic index is a blood glucose indicator, where *gly* = glucose, *emic* = blood and *index* = an indicator. This work of Jenkins disproved the assumption that equivalent amounts of carbohydrate from different foods caused similar glycemic responses. Furthermore, the researchers concluded that the carbohydrate exchange lists that have regulated the diets of most diabetic individuals do not reflect the physiological effect of foods and are therefore no longer sufficient to control blood glucose levels. With research done over the past three decades, scientists proved that it is not only the amount of carbohydrate but also its rate of digestion and absorption into the bloodstream – in other words, the GI – that determine the physiological response of the body. Research conducted all over the world since then confirms that the new way of ranking foods according to their actual effect on blood glucose is scientifically more accurate.

In a typical GI list, carbohydrate-rich foods are ranked on a scale from 1 to 100, according to their actual effect on blood glucose levels. Internationally, glucose is taken as 100, since it causes the greatest and most rapid rise in blood glucose levels, and all other foods are rated in comparison to glucose. It must be noted, however, that some published GI testing has used white bread as the reference food, which is completely acceptable in the scientific world, but could create the impression that certain GI values from different sources seem to differ. When looking up GI values, therefore, always establish whether the reference food used is glucose or bread. The *South African Glycemic Index and Load Guide* by Gabi Steenkamp and Liesbet Delport (Glycemic Index Foundation of South Africa [GIFSA] 2007) is one of the most reliable sources of the GI values of commonly eaten foods in South Africa. It is available from www.gifoundation.com, www.gabisteenkamp.co.za, your dietician, local bookstore, health shop or pharmacy. All the values published in the *GI-GL Guide* are based on glucose as the reference food, and this *Guide* contains the most recent GI values of carbohydrate-rich foods tested in South Africa and internationally. Since the GI is a ranking of foods based on the actual effect on blood glucose levels, instead of on assumptions, it is a much more accurate tool to use in the regulation of blood glucose levels.

Using the GI concept, diabetic individuals, those suffering from other blood glucose control problems and sportsmen and -women can all optimise their blood glucose control. Other blood glucose control problems are low blood sugar (hypoglycemia), hyperinsulinemia and insulin resistance, polycystic ovarian syndrome (PCOS), candidiasis, chronic fatigue syndrome (CFS), fibromyalgia syndrome (FMS) and attention deficit (hyperactivity) disorder (AD(H)D) in children. For a lower GI, lower fat recipe book for children, see *Sustained Energy for Kids* by Gabi Steenkamp, Tanzia Merlin and Jeske Wellmann (Tafelberg 2006). For detailed information for sportsmen and -women, see *Eat Smart for Sport* by Liesbet Delport and Dr Paula Volschenk (Tafelberg 2007).

Total and low density lipoprotein (LDL) cholesterol, and serum triglyceride levels and blood pressure can be lowered if the GI concept is used in combination with lower fat eating, and high density lipoprotein (HDL) cholesterol levels may be increased. HDL cholesterol is considered the "good" cholesterol. For those who want to lose weight, the increased satiety, and the fact that less insulin (a fat storer) is secreted, result in better fat loss. For a simple and comprehensive weight management book based on these principles, see *Eat Smart and Stay Slim: The GI Diet* by Liesbet Delport and Gabi Steenkamp (Tafelberg 2003).

Eating the low GI way and emphasising beneficial fats also protects from, and can be used to treat inflammatory conditions such as arthritis, gout and cancer.

For detailed information on different types of fat, see *The South African Fat and Protein Guide* by Prof Nola Dippenaar and Liesbet Delport (GIFSA 2006). Even people suffering from irritable bowel syndrome (IBS) can benefit from lower fat eating and the GI concept, although they, as well as those suffering from arthritis, gout and cancer, should consult a dietician, as some other adjustments will also have to be made to their diets. See www.gifoundation.com for a list of dieticians who use the GI concept. Foods with a low GI release glucose slowly and steadily into the bloodstream and do not over-stimulate insulin secretion. High insulin levels are implicated in many of the diseases of our modern lifestyle: high blood pressure, for instance, as well as high cholesterol and high triglyceride levels, diabetes, hypoglycemia, obesity, polycystic ovarian syndrome, coronary heart disease, arthritis, gout and cancer.

Apart from being lower GI, all the recipes in this book are also lower in fat, and the fats they do contain are mainly beneficial fats.

Fats, especially saturated fat and trans fatty acids, are the primary dietary cause of heart disease and high cholesterol, high blood pressure, excess weight and cancer, and these fats also play a major role in the development of hyper-insuline-mia, insulin resistance, diabetes, AD(H)D and gout. In contrast to this, beneficial fats such as mono-unsaturated fatty acids (MUFAs) and omega-3 poly-unsaturated fatty acids (PUFAs) protect against the development of many of the conditions mentioned above. A high fat intake aggravates irritable bowel syndrome and also results in insulin working less effectively, especially if the person is overweight and consumes mainly detrimental or "bad" fats, which may play a role in the development of hyperinsulinemia, insulin resistance and eventually diabetes.

Furthermore, it was found that it is fat (especially "bad" fat), and not really carbohydrate (starches, vegetables, fruit and sugars), that is fattening. This is especially the case if low GI carbohydrates are consumed most of the time and higher GI carbohydrates are reserved for during and/or after exercise. It takes no effort for the body to turn dietary fat into body fat, whereas it takes a great deal of effort and energy for the body to convert carbohydrate and protein into body fat. Thin people mostly consume a lower fat diet that is higher in carbohydrate and moderate in protein. Overweight people tend to eat high fat diets and/or diets that contain mainly high GI carbohydrate, while being inactive.

Not more than 30% of total energy in the diet should come from fat, and of this not more than one third should come from the less beneficial saturated and trans fats. However, the latter should preferably be avoided. In this book we have heeded this recommendation and have kept the fat content of every meal serving as close to 10 g of fat (or below) as possible, focusing mainly on beneficial fats.

How the GI is determined

The blood glucose response (BGR) to glucose or white bread (the reference foods) of at least 10 people per food tested is measured. This is done on two to three occasions for each person, and the average value is the BGR of that person. The BGR to glucose is given the value of 100, and when bread has been used as the reference food, it has to be calibrated against glucose. Glucose is absorbed quickly and generally causes the greatest and most rapid rise in blood glucose of all foods. The BGRs of all other carbohydrate foods are also measured by blood tests in the same 10 people per food tested, and rated in comparison to glucose for each person. The mean GI of the food for the group is allocated the GI value that can be applied to the general population. We could say that the GI of a food represents its blood glucose raising ability.

Often the GI of a given food is not what we would expect. For example, the GI of South African brown bread is 81, whereas the mean GI of sweetened low fat fruit yoghurt is only 33. For this reason, all carbohydrate-containing foods need to be tested in order for their GI to be determined. By guessing the GI of a food we could be far from the mark. The GI values of over 800 foods have been determined worldwide and more foods are being tested on a weekly basis, overseas as well as in South Africa. For a complete reference guide on the GI and GL values of foods commonly used in South Africa, see *The South African Glycemic Index and Load Guide* by Gabi Steenkamp and Liesbet Delport, available from www.gifoundation.com, www.gabisteenkamp.co.za, your dietician, local bookstore, health shop or pharmacy.

Factors that influence the GI

Ongoing studies are revealing that body responses to foods are much more complex than originally appreciated. The following factors influence our digestion and absorption of carbohydrates and thus the GI of carbohydrate-rich foods. The GI is a measure on a numerical scale of how carbohydrate-containing foods affect blood glucose levels.

The degree of starch gelatinisation

Gelatinisation of starches occurs when starchy food is exposed to liquid and/or heat as in cooking. When potatoes are boiled, the heat and water expand the hard, compact granules (which usually make raw potatoes difficult to digest) into swollen granules. Some granules even burst and free the individual starch molecules, making them easier to digest. Remember that starch is a string of glucose molecules. The same happens when a sauce is thickened with flour or cornflour. The water binds with the starch in the presence of heat and gelatinises the flour, making it easy to digest. For this reason many confectionery items that contain sugar have a lower GI than those without. The sugar binds with some of the water, preventing it from binding with the flour, thereby limiting gelatinisation. The less a starch is gelatinised, the more slowly it is digested and absorbed, and the lower the GI.

INTRODUCTION

Particle size

Intact grains such as whole wheat, whole corn, whole rye, whole oats (groats) and whole barley have much lower GI values than flours made from the same grains, because they have to be chewed and the enzymes of the body take longer to digest them.

Processing

Milling, beating, liquidising, grinding, mixing, mashing and re-fining foods raises the GI of the food by making it more easily available to the body. For this reason we limit the amount of beating and liquidising in the recipes. However, research has found that some food processing methods, such as parboiling of wheat and rice, may lower the glycemic response as it seems to reduce gelatinisation. That is why Spekko long grain parboiled rice, for example, has a low GI value.

The chemical composition of starch

Apart from the fact that processing methods can influence the GI values of starches, starches also have different structures, which affect their digestibility. Some types of rice, such as Basmati and Tastic, have a higher amylose content. Amylose is made up of long, straight chains of glucose molecules packed closely together, which exclude water and are therefore more difficult to digest. Other rice has a higher amylopectin content. The branched chains of amylopectin are more open, hydrate more easily, are much easier to digest and thus have a higher GI. Rice that contains predominantly amylose, like Tastic white rice, is inclined to be a loose cooked rice, whereas rice that contains predominantly amylopectin, like Arborio and Jasmine rice, tends to be a more sticky cooked rice.

The type and content of fibre

Foods containing soluble fibre – such as oat bran, minimally processed oats, legumes (beans, peas and lentils), citrus and deciduous fruits – have a GI-lowering effect, as they make the stomach contents more viscous and delay gastric emptying. Insoluble fibre such as that found in digestive bran, has little effect on the digestibility of the carbohydrate foods in which it is found. Thus, foods containing wheat (digestive) bran do not have a lower GI than foods without the bran, unless the digestive bran is used in large quantities, as in high fibre bran cereals. Brown bread and white bread have similar GI values, and so do refined and unrefined mealie-meal. However, some insoluble fibres, such as fibre found in sugar beet and *ispaghula*, do have a GI-lowering effect, as they have a greater water-holding capacity than digestive bran, which helps to slow down digestion.

Sugar (sucrose)

Sugar may lower the GI of foods that have a very high GI, because sugar has a lower GI than many refined starches. A good example of this is Rice Crispies, which has a high GI. When the cereal is sugar-coated, the GI is lower, and thus Strawberry Pops have a lower GI than Rice Crispies! Likewise, sugar-free Weetbix has a higher GI than regular Weetbix, which contains sugar. Sugar can also lower the GI of baked goods.

Protein and fat

The presence of fat and protein in food may lower the GI due to the interaction of these nutrients with each other and with the carbohydrate. Fat slows down the rate at which food leaves the stomach and protein leads to the secretion of insulin by the pancreas, without raising blood glucose levels, resulting in an overall lower glycemic response. However, it is not advisable to eat too much protein or fat. Protein tends to impair the body's ability to produce insulin, and fat (particularly saturated fat) has the effect of decreasing the effectiveness of insulin. Protein also overtaxes the kidneys, and an over-consumption of protein can lead to osteoporosis, arthritis and gout, and can aggravate heart disease.

Anti-nutrients

Phytates, lectins, saponins and polyphenols (tannins) normally slow digestion and thereby decrease the GI. These are normal constituents of many vegetables, legumes, fruit and bran.

Acidity

The more acid a food, the lower its GI, as acids slow the speed at which the stomach empties. For example, pickled beetroot has a lower GI than hot cooked beetroot. The more tart fruits also have slighty lower GI values. Sourdough breads, such as ciabatta, have a lower GI than regular bread, because of the acids formed which slow gastric emptying.

Cooking

Cooking increases the digestibility of food, which usually has the effect of raising the GI of that food.

Resistant starch (RS)

This type of starch resists digestion in the small intestine and passes into the large intestine, where it acts like fibre. It is fermented by the colonic microflora and promotes the synthesis of short chain fatty acids, which have many health benefits. There are three types of resistant starch:

- RS1 – whole or partly ground grains, seeds, cereals and legumes.
- RS2 – some raw starch granules, such as potato and green banana.
- RS3 – retrograded starch, which develops in some cooked and cooled starches, such as mealie-meal and samp. Thus cooked and cooled maize porridge has a lower GI than the hot, freshly prepared porridge, because the body has difficulty in digesting the retrograded starch that develops when some cooked starches are cooled.

Speed of eating

Studies have shown that our blood glucose levels rise less rapidly when we eat more slowly.

The glycemic load (GL)

A relatively new concept, called the glycemic load (GL), developed by scientists at Harvard University, USA, "fine tunes" the GI concept. It addresses the concern about rating carbohydrate foods as either "good" or "bad" on the basis of their GI. There is no such thing as a good or bad carbohydrate food – all foods can fit into a healthy diet, depending on when you eat them, how much you eat and with what you combine them. Although low GI food is usually the preferred choice, a high GI sports drink is perfect during and after extended exercise. A low GI drink during or after intense exercise could in fact result in hypoglycemia.

The GL of a specific food portion is an expression of how much impact that portion of food will have on blood glucose levels. It is the "glucose load" that the body has to deal with in order to keep blood glucose levels within normal limits. The GL is calculated by taking the carbohydrate content in a specific portion of food and multiplying it by its GI value, but because the GI is an index, the value obtained should be divided by 100, as shown in the following formula:

$$GL = \text{carbohydrate content of portion} \times \frac{GI}{100}$$

The GL is thus a measure that incorporates both the quantity (amount) and quality (GI) of the dietary carbohydrate consumed. Some fruits and vegetables, for example, have higher GI values and might be perceived as "bad". However, considering the amount of carbohydrate per portion, the GL is low. This means that their effect on blood glucose levels would be minimal.

Let us consider a few examples:
- The GI of **watermelon** is high (GI = 72), but the GL of one serving of watermelon (3 cm slice or 200 g) is reasonable (GL = 10). This is because the amount of carbohydrate in this serving size is small, as watermelon contains a lot of water. This does *not* hold true for watermelon juice, however, as it is a concentrated source of carbohydrate and consequently the quantity of carbohydrate therein is greater, giving a higher GL. The higher GL is due not only to the higher GI, but also to the more concentrated amount of carbohydrate in a glass of watermelon juice. Thus, bear in mind that *all* fruit juices are concentrated sources of carbohydrate and have higher GLs.
- The GI of **apples** is 38 and the GL of one medium apple is 7. This means that eating one apple will have little effect on blood glucose levels. However, if you eat a 500 g packet of dried apples, which is the equivalent of 14 fresh apples, the GL would be 98. This will have a significant effect on blood glucose levels, despite the snack being low GI, as dried fruit is a highly concentrated source of carbohydrate. The GL therefore shows us how important it is to watch portion sizes.

- The GI of our local **white or brown bread** is high (GI ⩾ 70) and the GL of two slices (two 40 g slices of bread contain 40 g of carbohydrate) is also high (GL > 30), because the amount of carbohydrate in bread is substantial. This means that a sandwich made with two slices of brown or white bread will have a marked effect on blood glucose levels, as the bread in the sandwich will have a GL of about 30. However, should you use one thin slice of bread as part of a mixed meal containing low GI baked beans, ham and other salad vegetables, the GL of the meal will be lower and more acceptable (GL = 22). Note that the two slices of refined bread on their own have a higher GL than a whole meal in which only one thin slice of bread is used in combination with other low GI foods.
- The GL of one slice of **seed loaf bread** is only about 9. The GL of a meal consisting of a sandwich made from heavier bread instead of brown or white bread, can be lowered from about 30 to about 20. This means that regular refined bread will spike blood glucose levels (higher GL), and the seed loaf will not (lower GL). But it does not mean that you can overindulge in lower GI breads.
- In addition, the GL of a **roll** (the equivalent of two slices of bread) is over 20, and the GL of a **bagel** (the equivalent of three slices of bread) is over 30. Imagine what this does to blood glucose levels, as the GI is also high.

These examples show us that it is quite acceptable to include small amounts of high GI foods in a meal, as long as the bulk of the meal contains lower GI carbohydrate foods such as vegetables, fruit, low GI starches, legumes and/or dairy.

New evidence associates a high GL diet with an increased risk of heart disease, cancer and diabetes, especially in overweight and insulin-resistant people. Therefore, it is advisable to restrict the GL of a typical meal to between 20 and 25 as far as possible, but definitely below 30. The GL of a typical snack should preferably be about 10, and definitely below 15, but if your meals are all close to 30, the total of all your snacks should be no more than 10. This means that you would have to eat only fruit for snacks, in order to keep your total daily GL below 100, as the GL of a portion of fruit is usually below 10. This applies primarily to overweight and diabetic individuals of medium height, who are not very active. If your weight is normal and/or you are quite young, or tall, and particularly if you are moderately active, your daily GL total should be closer to 110–120. The total daily GL of very active sportsmen and -women of normal weight should be more than 120.

What does it mean when a food has a low GL?

A carbohydrate food that has a low GL will have a small impact on blood glucose levels, as it is either not high in carbohydrate and/or has a low GI, so one would have to eat quite a lot of it before it would have any effect on blood glucose levels. Eating any one of the muffins contained in this book, or in *Eating for*

Sustained Energy 1 or *2*, *Sustained Energy for Kids* or *Snacks and Treats for Sustained Energy 1*, should not raise blood glucose levels significantly, as they all have a lower GL.

Having a **low GL and low GI** is doubly beneficial. A food with a low GI and GL will naturally have a very small impact on blood glucose levels. Such foods include low GI vegetables – asparagus, mushrooms, tomatoes, lettuce, cucumber, onions, and so on – and low GI fruits – apples, pears, peaches, berries, oranges, etc. Remember, the GI indicates the extent to which a food will raise blood glucose levels, whereas the GL indicates the "power" or "push" behind the GI.

High GI and high GL spells trouble – blood glucose levels will shoot up. This means the food in question will have a lot of "power" behind an already high GI, and even a small portion will have a marked effect. Examples of this are cooked mealie-meal and potatoes, and regular South African bread. These foods are concentrated sources of carbohydrate, and therefore even a small portion contains a lot of carbohydrate, pushing the GL up even further. In addition they have high GI values, which aggravate the effect on blood glucose levels.

Low GI combined with high GL will also have an impact on blood glucose levels. Remember that the GL is based on the quantity of carbohydrate in a food, and represents the GI (quality of carbohydrate) within a portion size. Thus, the more carbohydrate there is in a food, the higher its GL and the greater the impact on blood glucose levels. So even low GI foods, if eaten in large quantities, can affect blood glucose levels quite significantly, especially if they are concentrated sources of carbohydrates, such as most cakes, dried fruit and dried fruit rolls, fruit juices, crisps, chocolates, etc. Crisps and chocolates are also high in fat and/or saturated fat and trans fats, making them a much less healthy choice.

High GI combined with a low GL will not necessarily affect blood glucose levels significantly. A good example is higher GI melons. They are not very concentrated sources of carbohydrate and therefore, in **normal** portion sizes (1 cup melon cubes), will not impact on blood glucose levels even though they have a high GI. The proviso is that they are not eaten with other high GI or GL foods, and not in large quantities.

The GL of one serving of the starch component of most of our low GI breakfasts is about 15. The GL of one serving of the starch component of most low GI light meals in our recipe books is between 15 and 20. The GL of one serving of most low GI main meals is between 20 and 25. This means that three meals per day should add up to a GL of between 55 and 70, as most people will add salad and/or fruit to breakfasts and light meals, which also contribute to the GL. This leaves 30–45 GL for snacks and drinks. One serving of most of the snacks in our recipe books has a GL of 10–15. Fruit has a GL of below 10. The aim is to keep the total GL per day at around 100, especially for people with diabetes and other lifestyle diseases, and even more so for those who need to lose weight. For active and tall individuals the daily GL should be over 120.

How to make the GI work for you

All foods that have a GI of 55 or less are slow release carbohydrates and are the best choice for most people. This is particularly true for inactive people, the overweight, sportsmen and -women before exercise, and those suffering from diabetes, hypoglycemia, hyperinsulinemia, insulin resistance, candidiasis, PCOS, ME, FMS, inflammatory diseases such as arthritis, high triglycerides and AD(H)D. Slow release carbohydrates do not result in a sudden, high rise in blood glucose levels, and for this reason they keep blood glucose levels steady for several hours. They are called **low GI foods**. Low GI foods are more satisfying and do not cause the release of as much insulin as high GI foods, and therefore they also prevent the reactive drop in blood glucose levels. High GI foods elicit a huge insulin response – the body's way of coping with the sudden, sharp rise in blood glucose levels – after high GI foods have been eaten. Often, the insulin response is too great and blood glucose levels fall rapidly below the starting point – the condition known as hypoglycemia.

This swing from very high to very low blood glucose levels, due to hyperinsulinemia, is now believed to be a contributing factor to most of the so-called "lifestyle diseases". These diseases are actually caused by high insulin levels in the blood and could be prevented, to a large extent, if the general public were to consume lower fat, lower GI foods most of the time and reserve higher GI foods for during and/or after exercise. Researchers regard all foods with a GI of 62 or below as "safe", even though the theoretical cut-off point for a low GI food is 55.

Intermediate and high GI foods, on the other hand, are extremely useful for sportsmen and -women, during and after sport. Intermediate GI foods are those with a GI ranging from 56 to 69 and that release glucose into the bloodstream over a period of about two hours. They are the best choice after low-intensity exercise of short duration, and for those with diabetes, directly after moderate activity, or during and after exercise lasting more than one and a half hours.

Foods with a GI above 70 are fast release carbohydrates and are called **high GI foods**. High GI foods are excellent for the prevention of fatigue and hypoglycemia in healthy sportsmen and -women if consumed within 30–60 minutes after completing high intensity exercise. High GI drinks and foods are also useful during exercise lasting more than one and a half hours. However, any person wishing to have sustained energy during exercise should not consume high GI foods before exercise or when he or she is inactive, but rather have low GI foods. For detailed information on sports nutrition, see *Eat Smart for Sport* by Liesbet Delport and Dr Paula Volschenk (Tafelberg 2007).

Small quantities of high GI foods are also useful during a low blood glucose "attack" (the so-called "hypo"), but it is better to prevent a low blood glucose level than to treat it.

Healthy eating

In South Africa we now have the Food Based Dietary Guidelines, which are easy to understand and implement on a daily basis (see below). By simply applying the first guideline – eating a variety of foods at every meal – you ensure a wide range of nutrients, which in turn optimises nutrition. By applying all of the guidelines good nutrition is ensured, and the recipes in all our books do just that.

The South African Dietary Guidelines
- Enjoy a variety of foods.
- Be active.
- Make lower GI starchy foods the basis of most meals.
- Eat plenty of vegetables and fruits every day.
- Eat cooked dry beans, peas, lentils and soya regularly.
- Eat lower fat chicken, fish, meat, milk, yoghurt, cheese or eggs daily.
- Eat fats, especially saturated fats, sparingly and try to avoid trans fats.
- Use salt and eat salty foods sparingly.
- Drink lots of clean, safe water.
- If you drink alcohol, drink sensibly, that is, not more than one to two drinks per day.
- Eat and drink foods containing sugar sparingly, and not between meals.

Breakfast

Breakfast is the most important meal – it "sets the stage" for the rest of the day. This is particularly true for people with diabetes. A well-balanced, lower GI, lower fat breakfast stabilises blood glucose levels, so that when it is time for lunch, one is only just hungry and has not had a blood glucose surge or slump during the morning. In other words, the body has been able to operate with optimum fuel levels all morning. A high GI breakfast can result in shakiness, fatigue and irritability throughout the day, unless a substantial amount of exercise was done beforehand.

Breakfast should contain lower GI carbohydrate foods, such as a lower GI muffin or cereal or porridge (see the GI list on page 20), some protein, like lower fat cheese, and a little fat (which is already contained in the muffin and cheese). Fruit can either be added to the breakfast or eaten as a mid-morning snack. See pages 22–29 for breakfast ideas.

Lunch or light meals

Often, people tend not to eat lunch. This leads to very low blood glucose levels before suppertime, and often the result is an urge to raid the fridge. We would like to emphasise the importance of eating a lower fat, lower GI lunch, consisting mainly of lower GI foods such as salad vegetables with one or two slices of seed loaf (see the GI list on page 20 for more lower GI options). Add to this a little lower fat protein or dairy, such as lean meat, fish, chicken, cheese, eggs or legumes, and a minimum of fat, such as spreading avocado or peanut butter on the bread instead of margarine. Low GI fruit can conclude the meal, or be kept for a snack later. For lunch suggestions, see the sections on light meals (page 48), salads (page 38) and soups (page 30).

Supper, dinner or main meals

The bulk of the evening meal should, once again, be lower GI foods, in the form of vegetables and a small portion of starch. Approximately half the plate should be filled with vegetables, a quarter with low GI starch (see the GI list on page 20) and the remaining quarter with lower fat protein, such as lean meat, fish or chicken, or beans, peas, lentils or texturised vegetable protein. Vegetarians can use low fat milk, yoghurt, cheese, legumes or nuts as protein. However, nuts are 50% fat and their intake should be limited, even though they contain mainly healthier fat. See the sections on main meals (from page 56) and light meals (page 48).

Eating high GI carbohydrate for supper, after a day of non-activity, could result in reactive low blood glucose levels a few hours later or during the night. People with diabetes who eat high GI starches for supper will invariably have blood glucose levels elevated above 10 mmol/l about one hour after supper, and elevated fasting blood glucose levels over 7 mmol/l, the next morning – both of which are undesirable. Eating protein with higher GI carbohydrate will reduce the effect of the carbohydrate on blood glucose levels, but not as effectively as eating low GI carbohydrates instead. Eating large portions of protein and fat, such as fatty red meat, can also result in high blood glucose levels the next morning, especially in those who have diabetes. A high fat (particularly trans and saturated fat) diet also increases the risk for cardiovascular disease and weight gain.

Fibre

Most South Africans do not come close to eating the recommended 30–40 g of fibre per day. Low fibre intakes have been linked to high cholesterol levels, high blood pressure, diabetes (since most high fibre foods, though not all, are also low GI and, in addition, fibre improves insulin sensitivity), spastic colon, gallstones and cancer, especially colon and breast cancer.

Fibre is the indigestible part of plant foods, and is therefore not found in animal protein or fats. It moves almost untouched through the alimentary canal until it reaches the colon, adding bulk and softness to the stool for easy evacuation. There are two types of fibre: **water-soluble fibre** found in oats, oat bran, barley, legumes, pasta, mealies, deciduous and citrus fruits, some vegetables, and products high in vegetable gums, such as guar gum and carrageenan (found in edible red seaweed); and **insoluble fibre**, found in digestive bran, brown and whole wheat bread, whole wheat (sold as Weet-rice or pearled wheat), brown rice, etc. *Both* types of fibre play a vital role in gut health and should be consumed every day.

Foods that contain mostly soluble fibre also have a low GI. If eaten regularly, instead of high fat, high GI foods, they can protect against type 2 diabetes, since these foods do not over-stimulate insulin secretion. Soluble fibre also binds cholesterol and is therefore effective in lowering cholesterol levels. Constant over-stimulation of insulin secretion by eating high GI, low fibre foods may lead to the depletion of the beta cells of the pancreas, which are responsible for insulin production, and the onset of type 2 diabetes. Eating a high fat (especially trans and saturated fat) diet makes insulin work less effectively, predisposing people to insulin resistance.

Although we do include some low fibre foods in the GI list on pages 20 and 21 – so that you can see which foods are low, intermediate and high GI – we want to encourage you to choose higher fibre products that are also lower in fat and GI, instead of the refined counterpart.

The sweet truth about sugar

When we hear the word "sugar", we automatically think of table sugar – the sweetness we add to tea and coffee. There is much more to sugar than that. Chemically, sugar is known as sucrose, but technically there are many types of sugar. The sugar in fruit, for example, can be fructose, sucrose, glucose or a combination of any of these; the sugar in milk is known as lactose; and so on. A sugar free food may, in fact, not be sugar free at all – merely free of sucrose – and not necessarily low GI or lower in kilojoules (kJ). New South African legislation may not allow for a food to be called "sugar free" if it contains any one of the various types of sugars listed below, unless the GI has been tested.

The various types of sugars are:

- **Sugars:**
  - *Mono-* and *disaccharides:* These consist of either one or two molecules of different sugars and have varying effects on blood glucose levels or the GI of the food containing them. Some (low GI) are absorbed more slowly and steadily, while others (high GI) can be absorbed rapidly.
  - *Fructose*, also known as Krystar 300, Fructofin C (fructose – GMO free), Dolcresun Q0 and Q2 (a syrup very high in fructose), and *lactose* (milk sugar) each have a low GI, but contain as many kJ as table sugar.
  - *Sucrose* (table sugar) and *invert sugar* have an intermediate GI and contain as many kJ as the above.
  - *Glucose, dextrose, maltose* and *maltotriose* are high GI and contain as many kJ as table sugar.
- **Sugar alcohols/polyols:** These also consist of two molecules of different sugars, and in addition are bound to an alcohol molecule. This makes them more difficult to digest, which means the sugar is released into the bloodstream more slowly, resulting in a low GI value. A certain percentage of these sugars is not digested at all, and thus they contain fewer kJ than regular sugars. However, they can cause gastric discomfort – flatulence, cramping and/or diarrhoea – if taken in excess. Examples of sugar alcohols are *lactitol, xylitol, isomalt, maltitol, sorbitol* and *mannitol.*

- **Oligosaccharides:** These consist of three to nine molecules, with two or more different sugars, and can be either low or high GI.
  - *Indigestible oligosaccharides* (low GI) are not digested at all, and the body deals with them as it does with fibre. All of them are therefore low GI and most are also kJ free, except for Sugalite, which contains about a third of the kJ of table sugar. These sugars ferment in the colon and form short chain fatty acids. This has certain health benefits, such as a reduction in fasting blood glucose, but they can also cause gastric discomfort – flatulence, cramping and/or diarrhoea – if taken in excess. Examples of oligosaccharides include Frutafit HD, IQ and TEX, Inulin (FOS or fructo-oligosaccharides), polydextrose, Litesse Ultra (ultra-refined polydextrose), Litesse II (refined polydextrose), pyrodextrins, galacto-oligosaccharides, raffinose, stachyose and Sugalite.
  - *Malto-oligosaccharides* (high GI), such as maltodextrin, are easily digested and contain as many kJ as table sugar and have a very high GI value – over 100!
- **Polysaccharides:** These consist of more than 10 molecules and contain as many kJ as table sugar, and most of them are high GI as well. Examples of these are *dextrins* – intermediate products in the hydrolysis of starch – and consist of shorter chains of glucose units, and *glucose polymers* or *corn syrup solids*, which are partially or fully hydrolysed cornstarch.
- **Non-nutritive or artificial sweeteners:** These are the only sweeteners that are virtually free of energy or kJ. Do not eat them too freely as we are not sure of their long-term effects on the human body. Examples include *saccharine, cyclamates, acesulfame K, aspartame* and *sucralose.*

Now you know how to distinguish between the effects of different "sugars" on blood glucose levels, as well as their energy values. If any of the high GI "sugars" listed above is one of the first three ingredients in a product, beware – the GI might just be high!

Conditions that benefit from the lower GI, lower fat way of eating

Diabetes mellitus

Diabetes is on the increase at a rate of 11% per year, and there is talk of an "epidemic" of diabetes. This is partly due to the high GI, high fat (particularly trans and saturated fat) diet the general public consumes, as well as an increasingly sedentary lifestyle, stress and smoking.

There are two types of diabetes: type 1 diabetes (10% of diabetics) and type 2 diabetes (90% of diabetics). In **type 1 diabetes**, the beta cells of the pancreas are unable to produce insulin and the onset is usually sudden. A pre-existing genetic component is usually present, as well as a precipitating factor, for example a viral infection or, in some cases, certain proteins sparking off an immune response. Often it is the trigger that is the proverbial last straw for the person developing diabetes. However, these do not *cause* diabetes. The classic symptoms, especially of type 1 diabetes, include chronic thirst, chronic urination, chronic hunger and excessive weight loss, in spite of the person consuming large quantities of food and drink. People with type 1 diabetes need to inject insulin every day.

Type 2 diabetes is less easy to diagnose and the onset is usually slow. Thirty percent of those with type 2 diabetes already have complications at the time of diagnosis. Usually, these people are overweight, have insulin resistance and have high cholesterol and/or high triglycerides, as well as high blood pressure. They often have no, or vague, symptoms, for example chronic infections, chronic fatigue, pain, cramps or a burning sensation in the legs and feet, shortness of breath, visual problems, etc. Some have a relative insulin deficiency and can be treated with diet and exercise alone, or with diet, exercise and medication. Others have an absolute insulin shortage and need to be treated with diet, exercise and insulin therapy. Early diagnosis is important, so have your blood glucose, blood lipids and blood pressure checked regularly, irrespective of symptoms. The earlier diabetes is diagnosed and treated, the smaller the chances of serious complications, such as blindness, kidney failure, amputations, heart attacks or stroke.

Modern treatment of diabetes

As with all new research, the GI has not been universally welcomed. Most of its critics cling to past assumptions. Unfortunately, they prefer to believe what they think should happen to blood glucose in response to eating certain foods, rather than what actually happens to blood glucose when carbohydrate foods are eaten. Remember that the GI is a physiological measure of the body's response to a particular carbohydrate-containing food.

Research conducted over the past 30 years in Canada, Australia, the United Kingdom, Italy, France, Denmark, the East and Far East, as well as South Africa, shows convincingly that many foods that were regarded as "safe" in the traditional sugar free diet actually raise blood glucose levels higher than some ordinary foods that may contain a little sugar. Some of the foods previously regarded as "safe" are now found to elicit very high blood glucose levels, and thus should rather be avoided. Many other foods that contain sugar, which people with diabetes have been encouraged to avoid in the past, cause no major fluctuations in blood glucose levels. It does not, therefore, make sense to ban these foods for individuals with diabetes. If you consult the GI list on pages 20 and 21, you will notice that South African brown bread has a high GI value, whereas sweetened fruit yoghurt has a low GI value. This means that one or two slices of brown bread, eaten as dry toast, for example, would result in a much greater increase in blood glucose levels than would eating a small tub of sweetened fruit yoghurt.

The new lower fat, lower GI diet is much more effective in lowering and controlling blood glucose levels, because it is based on what happens to real people (healthy people and those with diabetes) when they eat real food, in real life. Dieticians across the world have many examples of how diabetic individuals' insulin and oral medication was decreased – or even discontinued in some cases – since starting a lower GI, lower fat diet. Many had been on a sugar free diet (and sometimes even low fat as well) for many years and still could not get their blood glucose readings under 10 mmol/l. As soon as they started following the lower fat, lower GI diet, their readings dropped to below 10 mmol/l. They achieved this not by avoiding sugar, but by avoiding high fat, high GI foods.

A high fat (particularly trans and saturated fat) diet also results in the insulin working less effectively, which in turn can lead to a relative or absolute shortage of insulin, as well as hyperinsulinemia and insulin resistance. This predisposes to all the lifestyle diseases – diabetes, heart disease, hypertension, excessive weight and even cancer. The lower fat, lower GI diet is much more user friendly than the traditional diabetic diet because sugar is no longer completely forbidden.

Portion control is also easier when slow release (lower GI), lower fat foods are involved, as the increased satiety helps to control how much is eaten. If you are overweight, however, you will have to watch portion sizes more carefully. For this reason, we give the number of portions of starch, protein, fat, etc., per serving for every recipe, so that those who want or need to watch their weight can do so by sticking to the recommended number of portions given to them by a dietician. In addition, keeping to the number of servings recommended per dish, provided at the start of every recipe, will help anyone involved in weight management. Larger portion sizes, however, are also acceptable for those whose weight is normal or who need to carbo-load or gain weight.

All the recipes in our books are suitable for people with diabetes. Every meal consumed by a diabetic individual should contain at least one low GI (slow release) food. If most of the foods in a meal are low GI, then intermediate and even small amounts of high GI foods can be added to the meal. We applied this principle in many of the recipes in this book, and mention this in the Dieticians' notes. For maximum reduction in blood glucose levels – especially if you have a fasting blood glucose value that is higher than 8 mmol/l and a random blood glucose that is higher than 10 mmol/l – consumption of low GI foods at every meal becomes vitally important.

Hypoglycemia

Hypoglycemia, or low blood sugar, is a condition in which blood glucose levels fall below normal; *hypo* = under and *glycemia* = blood sugar/glucose. Not surprisingly, many people suffer from hypoglycemia, since most of the foods that are freely available and consumed by the general public are high in fat and have a high GI.

The most common form of hypoglycemia occurs after a

meal or snack is eaten. This is called **reactive hypoglycemia**. Except when eaten during or after exercise, high GI foods result in a sharp increase in blood glucose levels within a short period of time, 15–30 minutes after ingestion. The body then tries to rectify the situation by releasing insulin to counteract the threat of sustained high blood glucose levels. Insulin removes the glucose from the bloodstream too enthusiastically, resulting in a rapid fall in blood glucose levels. The result is the collection of typical stress-like symptoms of low blood sugar, such as tremors, heart palpitations, sweating, anxiety, irritability, sleepiness, weakness and shakiness, as well as chronic fatigue. Hypoglycemia can also affect mental function and lead to restlessness, irritability, poor concentration, visual disturbance, lethargy and drowsiness. These symptoms are clearly noticeable during research conducted on non-diabetic people who eat high GI foods.

The logical treatment for hypoglycemia is to control the influx of glucose into the bloodstream. By consuming mainly slow release carbohydrate foods (low GI) at mealtimes and as snacks, a slow but steady stream of glucose is released into the bloodstream, which will not trigger the release of huge surges of insulin. If eating high GI and high fat (especially trans and saturated fat) foods, it is only a question of time before impaired glucose tolerance develops. This is the forerunner of type 2 diabetes, and it occurs because the beta cells of the pancreas (which produce insulin) become worn out by continually trying to correct the surges of glucose released into the blood when fast release foods (high GI) are eaten, and the insulin that is released cannot work properly due to the high fat diet.

This can lead to hyperinsulinemia, which is too much insulin in the blood in response to the high blood glucose levels, and insulin resistance. Hyperinsulinemia results in cells shutting down and becoming resistant to the working of insulin. Cells cannot function while being "drowned" in insulin and "forget" to absorb the glucose from the bloodstream in response to insulin. The result is high insulin *and* high blood glucose levels.

Other factors that contribute to insulin resistance are genetic factors, inactivity, obesity and ageing. Hyperinsulinemia can lead to diabetes, hyperlipidemia, hypertension and heart disease, as well as resistant excessive weight or obesity. This entire vicious cycle needs to be broken before the body will start functioning properly again.

Follow these simple guidelines to prevent hypoglycemia and its consequences:
- Eat regular meals and snacks, preferably every three hours.
- Include slow release carbohydrate foods (low GI) in every meal or snack to keep blood glucose levels steady.
- Avoid eating fast release foods (high GI) on their own. Preferably avoid them altogether (see the GI list on page 21). Small amounts of high GI carbohydrate should be combined with a low GI carbohydrate food or some protein or a little beneficial fat. Eating high and low GI foods together yields an overall intermediate GI. For tips on food-combining, see *The South African Glycemic Index and Load Guide* by Gabi Steenkamp

and Liesbet Delport (GIFSA 2007), available from www.gifoundation.com, www.gabisteenkamp.co.za, your dietician, local bookstore, health shop or pharmacy.

Sport-induced hypoglycemia

Hypoglycemia occurring during or after sport is the result of consuming nothing, or fast release (high GI) carbohydrates before exercise. It can also happen when nothing or slow release carbohydrates are eaten or drunk during and/or after exercise, and when food is not eaten immediately after exercise of long duration.

To prevent this, low GI (slow release) carbohydrate foods should be consumed one to two hours before exercise. Consuming higher GI, fast release beverages or food during and within 30–60 minutes after exercise lasting more than one and a half hours, keeps blood glucose levels steady and replenishes glycogen used by the muscles. For detailed information on sports nutrition, see *Eat Smart for Sport* by Liesbet Delport and Dr Paula Volschenk (Tafelberg 2007).

Coronary heart disease

In Westernised South Africans, 40% of deaths in the economically active age group result from chronic diseases of lifestyle, such as cancer, hypertension (high blood pressure), diabetes, stroke and coronary heart disease (CHD). Of all of these, CHD causes the greatest number of deaths.

CHD develops slowly, and the process begins with fatty deposit build-up on the inner walls of the arteries. This leads to narrowing of the arteries (artherosclerosis) that supply the heart and the brain with oxygen.

When blood flow is impeded, the person suffers a heart attack or stroke. Often, a part of the heart muscle dies or a part of the body is paralysed (stroke). Excess cholesterol slowly constricts and clogs arteries without pain or discomfort, except maybe fatigue and shortness of breath. Some people experience chest pain (angina), but for many, the first warning sign is the heart attack or stroke.

Risk factors

Several factors contribute to an increased risk of CHD, including high cholesterol, high blood pressure, excessive weight, diabetes, smoking, stress, lack of exercise and a family history of CHD. These are all influenced by the quantity of fat (especially trans, saturated and "processed" fat) in the diet.

Higher trans and saturated fat intake results in more LDL cholesterol – the dangerous cholesterol. Oxidised LDL cholesterol is laid down in the arteries most easily and that is why it's important to prevent oxidation of LDL cholesterol by eating lots of fresh fruit and vegetables. Saturated fat encourages the body to make more cholesterol. This makes saturated fat the culprit in raising blood cholesterol levels and not dietary cholesterol, as was previously thought. Trans fat can reduce levels of the "good" HDL cholesterol, which is another reason why it should be avoided.

Fat, particularly trans and saturated fat, is also believed to be the main dietary promoter of cancer, as well as the main cause of extra body fat or obesity. Fatty meat such as lamb and mutton chops, dried sausage, fatty biltong, toasted sandwiches, pies and other confectionery such as cakes, tarts, biscuits, rusks and croissants, full cream ice cream, chocolate, rich sauces, desserts, hard margarine and all deep-fried foods are high in saturated and trans fats. Too much sodium, together with a high fat, high GI diet, too much alcohol, smoking and weight, and inactivity can all aggravate high blood pressure and the risk for CHD.

Treatment

It is possible to eat most foods, provided one chooses or makes the lower fat (particularly saturated and trans fat), lower GI and lower sodium version. This book is full of delicious recipes that are low in total fat, saturated fat, trans fatty acids, GI, GL and sodium, and will not cause fatty deposit build-up on the inner walls of arteries.

We recommend the use of canola or olive oil (which are both high in mono-unsaturated fatty acids, or MUFAs) as research has shown that large quantities of omega-6 poly-unsaturated fatty acids (PUFAs), especially from plant origin – for example, poly-unsaturated soft margarine, sunflower oil, cottonseed oil, etc. – can give rise to reactive chemicals called **free radicals**, which are implicated in heart disease, cancer and ageing, and can decrease the more beneficial HDL cholesterol.

PUFAs, which occur in fatty fish (omega-3s), such as pilchards, trout, tuna (in water or brine), sardines (without the oil), salmon and mackerel (in water), are healthier since they lower fibrinogen levels in the blood. This slows blood clotting, and also helps to increase the good HDL cholesterol. We recommend that fatty fish be eaten once, but preferably twice a week. For those who do not eat fish, canola and linseed or flax oil, as well as linseeds themselves, are plant sources of omega-3 fats.

MUFAs, found in olive oil, canola oil, macadamia oil, olives, avocados, peanut butter and raw unsalted nuts (except brazil nuts), decrease bad LDL cholesterol and raise good HDL cholesterol levels. HDL cholesterol is responsible for the removal of the "bad" fats from the arteries, by transporting them to the liver to be excreted. HDL cholesterol levels may be increased by exercise, a low GI diet containing mainly MUFAs and omega-3 fats, and wise consumption of red wine (one small glass of wine per day).

Fibre, especially soluble fibre (found in many low GI foods, such as legumes, barley and oat bran) also plays an important role in decreasing the risk of CHD. Soluble fibre binds cholesterol in the alimentary canal, thereby reducing serum cholesterol, particularly LDL cholesterol. For this reason, we have included recipes with one or other legume or lower GI oats/oat bran as an ingredient. The plant sterols in legumes are highly effective at decreasing the risk of heart disease, and oat products are the richest sources of soluble fibre.

To reduce the risk of CHD, exercise more, stop smoking, decrease your salt intake, lose weight or avoid becoming overweight and eat a lower fat, lower GI diet.

Attention deficit hyperactivity disorder (ADHD) or attention deficit disorder (ADD)

For years it was believed that ADHD and ADD were caused, or at least aggravated, by the consumption of sugar. Sugar was also believed to cause hypoglycemia, and it was recently found that hyperactivity and/or AD(H)D and hypoglycemia are interrelated. Now that we know it is high GI foods that cause hypoglycemia, we recommend that children who suffer from ADHD or ADD should avoid high GI foods – such as refined bread, most refined breakfast cereals, cold drinks, energy drinks and sweets that are high in glucose – rather than just avoiding foods that are high in sugar.

AD(H)D and hypoglycemia interrelation

Many children with ADHD or ADD crave fast release (high GI) foods. All high GI foods cause a rapid rise in blood glucose levels, which result in the pancreas pouring out insulin in an attempt to bring the blood glucose down to a normal level. In many people, and some children who suffer from ADHD or ADD, the body pours out too much insulin, resulting in excessive glucose being drawn out of the blood and the blood sugar level then falling below normal. The result is a hypoglycemic attack with the accompanying irritability, poor sleeping habits and lack of concentration. See the section on hypoglycemia, page 13, for other symptoms.

When high GI foods are eaten for breakfast, a hypoglycemic attack may occur one to one and half hours later – before first break at school, and at a time when the child should be concentrating, but now cannot as his or her blood glucose levels have dropped sharply. Had the child eaten a low GI breakfast, the brain would have received a steady supply of energy throughout the morning. If high GI foods are eaten at break (which happens often, since the child feels the need to compensate for the tired feeling by eating another high GI food), the scenario will be repeated later in the morning. This, we think, is the reason for these children struggling to concentrate. The brain's fuel is constantly undergoing huge swings, and this is not conducive to thinking or behaving in a normal manner.

Caffeine can also cause hyperactivity initially, and hypoglycemia with the resultant symptoms later. This is due to the stimulating effect of caffeine on the adrenal glands to excrete adrenalin, which stimulates the liver to pour glucose into the bloodstream. This sudden rise in blood sugar levels can once again cause the pancreas to pour out insulin. The result is a hypoglycemic attack.

Treatment

In light of the above, we recommend that high GI foods, caffeine and any food to which a child with ADHD or ADD is allergic should be avoided, as all these foods may induce

INTRODUCTION

hypoglycemia. If low GI foods are eaten most of the time, and particularly at breakfast (since breakfast sets the tone for the rest of the day), the brain receives a steady supply of energy. This is because low GI foods result in neither a sudden nor a substantial rise in blood glucose levels, and consequently there is no sudden drop in blood glucose levels due to the over-secretion of insulin. Low GI foods keep blood glucose levels even, enabling the child to concentrate better. Examples of low GI breakfast foods are lower GI oats, whole wheat Pronutro, high fibre cereal, deciduous fruits and fruit yoghurt, to name but a few. See the GI list on page 20 and the breakfast section on pages 22–29 for more ideas.

It is also advisable to keep the food for these children flavour-ant, preservative and colourant free. Colourants, in particular, have been found to inhibit the uptake of an important neuro-transmitter, vital for the transmission of messages. Foods and medicines containing salicylates may also have to be avoided, since they too can interfere with the transmission of messag-es in the brain. Moreover, these children benefit greatly from additional essential fatty acids (especially omega-3, which en-hances the transfer of messages in the brain), as well as certain vitamins and minerals. For more information, consult a dieti-cian who specialises in the treatment of AD(H)D and ADD. See GIFSA's website at www.gifoundation.com for a list of dieti-cians who use the GI in their treatment of patients.

The only exception to the low GI rule is during endurance ex-ercise and after all exercise. There is more about this in the sec-tion on sports nutrition (see page 17). The recipes in our books are suitable for children with ADHD and ADD, provided that the child does not suffer from an allergy to one of the ingredients, and is not salicylate sensitive.

Weight management

Follow a lower fat diet

Inexplicably, carbohydrate has been labelled as "fattening". Although research done in the last 15 to 20 years has disproved this again and again, carbohydrate is still struggling to get rid of this label. In fact, carbohydrate has been found to stimulate its own metabolism, which means that if you eat more of it, your body will merely burn more. However, this is *not* the case with fat. Dietary fat, and in particular saturated and trans fats, has been found to simply slip into body fat unchanged, indicating that it does not stimulate its own metabolism. Research has found that when eating a lot of a certain type of fat (such as that in chocolate), the fat in the body will look a lot like chocolate fat. Similarly, if a lot of cheese is eaten, the fat in the body will look a lot like the fat in cheese.

In a British study, scientists isolated several people in a room for a week, allowing them to eat low fat or fat free carbohy-drates to their hearts' content. After the week, these people had gained only a maximum of 1.5 kg. When these people were isolated and allowed to eat high fat foods in unlimited quantities,

some of the people picked up as much as 7 kg! This shows clearly that in order to lose weight (or rather fat), we need to cut down on our intake of visible and hidden fats. Fat is also energy dense as it contains 38 kJ/g, whereas carbohydrate and protein both contain only 17 kJ/g. All the recipes in our recipe books are much lower in fat than traditional recipes, and we also show, in the choice of ingredients and preparation methods, how to decrease the fat content of all meals and snacks. Do not, however, avoid fat altogether. A small quantity of beneficial fat is essential. This is necessary for the favourable effect on blood lipids, the skin and overall health, as well as preventing cravings.

Eat regular, small meals

Regular, smaller, snack-type meals are recommended for those who wish to lose weight and stay slim. Do not, however, end up eating all the time! Increased insulin secretion is stimulated when large meals are eaten, and insulin enhances fat stor-age. Hyperinsulinemia (too much insulin) is a major contributor to excessive weight, high body fat levels and the inability to lose weight. To facilitate weight loss and weight maintenance, excessive insulin secretion must be prevented. Food intake should not be cut too drastically, as energy levels below 4 200 kJ per day usually lead to a slowing of the metabolism. Less is not always best!

Eat lower GI foods

Another important aspect of weight loss is to keep blood glucose levels as stable as possible, and the best way to do this is to implement the concept of the GI. In a South African study – reported in *The GI Factor*, by Associate Professor Jenny Brand Miller, Kaye Foster-Powell and Dr Stephen Colagiuri (Hodder and Stoughton 1996) – it was found that insulin resist-ant female subjects who were placed on a low GI slimming diet lost 2 kg more weight over a period of 12 weeks than did their counterparts on a high GI diet. What was astounding was that both groups were given the identical quantity of fat, kilojoules, protein, carbohydrate and fibre. The success of the low GI slim-ming diet was attributed to the fact that such a diet does not cause a major insulin response, resulting in lower insulin levels and more stable blood glucose levels. This, in turn, assists the body in losing body fat, which is prevented by high insulin levels. In addition, low GI carbohydrates satisfy for longer, and prevent those "sweet cravings".

Exercise regularly

Regular exercise is an essential part of good health, and es-pecially relevant in successful weight management. In fact, it is so important that the South African Dietary Guidelines (see page 11) place exercise second on the list, even though it is not, strictly speaking, a dietary guideline. Exercise increases lean body mass, which in turn increases metabolism. Slimming without regular exercise can lead to muscle loss, because the body finds it easier to turn muscle into energy than to burn body fat for energy. This results in a slowing of the metabolism. This is particularly true if the food intake is cut drastically.

Your eating plan for weight management must be one you can follow for the rest of your life. Watch portion sizes, exercise regularly and be patient: it takes time to burn fat!

Find out why you eat

If you eat for emotional, physical or circumstantial reasons, instead of in response to your body needs – true hunger – tackle these obstacles first to optimise your success. Our book, *Eat Smart and Stay Slim: The GI Diet*, is a resource for more information on effective weight management.

Sports nutrition

The only exception to the low GI guideline applies during and after exercise. Generally speaking, to sustain energy, low GI carbohydrate foods should be eaten most of the time. Sportsmen and -women, however, should eat only low GI foods one to two hours before exercise, and resume low GI eating only a couple of hours after completing the exercise, depending on its duration and intensity. It is best to consume fast release, high GI foods and drinks immediately after exercise lasting about an hour, and during and immediately after exercise lasting more than 60-90 minutes, as well as for a few hours after endurance exercise, once again depending on the duration and intensity. Intermediate GI foods and drinks during and/or after exercise are recommended for the diabetic sportsman or -woman, and for those who have blood sugar (glucose) sensitivity.

Pre-sport or event

About 1 g of slow release, low GI carbohydrate per 1 kg of body weight should be consumed one to two hours before exercise. Low GI foods and drinks release glucose slowly and steadily, maintaining a healthy "petrol" level during the activity or sporting event.

During the event

Competitions or training sessions that last for more than one hour require fast release, high GI foods and drinks (intermediate GI for those with diabetes) at a rate of 30–60 g of carbohydrate per hour, depending on body weight and intensity of the exercise. If the duration of the exercise is less than 90 minutes, the low GI food or drink that was taken beforehand should be sufficient to sustain blood glucose at a healthy level and only water needs be consumed, at a rate of ±500 ml per hour.

Post-sport or event

It is crucial to consume at least 1 g of fast release, high GI (intermediate GI for those with diabetes) carbohydrate per 1 kg of body mass within the first 30–60 minutes after completing exercise, together with some protein. If the exercise lasts longer than 60–90 minutes, 1 g of high GI carbohydrate per 1 kg of body mass should be consumed immediately after, and again two hours later. Exercised muscles continue to absorb glucose from the bloodstream at the fastest rate during the first 30–60 minutes after exercise. The replenishment of glycogen into the fatigued muscle is faster if higher GI products are consumed as soon as possible after exercise ends, due to the action of the enzyme glycogen synthase. Doing this prevents severe hypoglycemia and ensures sustained energy levels and replenished glycogen levels in the muscles and liver. Consuming some protein with the carbohydrate directly after exercise will ensure full body muscle recovery.

For highly active people (those who train two to three hours every day) intermediate to high GI foods may have to be eaten most of the time, because of the sustained raised metabolism. However, if training is scaled down before an event, slow release or low GI carbohydrates should dominate all meals for the best carbo-loading effect. Carbo-loading can enhance performance in some people, but not in all. It is a good idea to try out any dietary changes long before the event to prevent any gastro-intestinal discomfort that may result from the higher carbohydrate diet during the three days before competing.

The recipes in this book are all lower GI and suitable for daily consumption. Sportsmen and -women who need high GI meals after their sports activity can substitute a high GI ingredient for a low GI ingredient in most of these recipes to convert the meal into a low fat, higher GI meal. For example, higher GI rice or high GI potatoes may be used instead of lower GI rice. Sportspeople should still eat lower fat meals, but fast release, high GI foods are required during and for a few hours after exercise, depending on its duration and intensity. For detailed information on sports nutrition, see *Eat Smart for Sport* by Liesbet Delport and Dr Paula Volschenk (Tafelberg 2007).

The vegetarian diet

This book is also suitable for vegetarians. All the recipes – except for a few main courses and light meals that contain meat, fish or chicken – are suitable, as many of these meals can be turned into vegetarian dishes simply by replacing the meat, fish or chicken with one to two tins of beans. One tin of cooked dry beans is equivalent to 250 ml or 1 cup of home cooked dry beans.

We have included a small vegetarian section to teach the inexperienced vegetarian how to incorporate beans and legumes in a tasty way, without the beans dominating the meal, and ensuring at the same time that the meals are nutritionally balanced. A large percentage of the vegetarian dishes in most recipe books are high in fat. We limited the quantity of cheese and other sources of hidden fat in our recipes to ensure that every recipe complied with our lower fat recommendations.

INTRODUCTION

The nutritional analysis of the recipes

Each recipe is accompanied by a box containing nutritional information. Most of the values are rounded off to the nearest whole number. Each box contains the following information and reflects the amounts per serving:

- The **GI** is a calculated value. The tested value will probably be lower, due to the interaction of the different nutrients. The GI gives an indication of how quickly, and by how much, the food will affect blood glucose levels.
- The **carbohydrate** (g) value gives the total carbohydrate content per serving, and includes the carbohydrate present in the dairy, starch, sweet ingredients (like sugar), vegetables and fruit.
- The **protein** (g) measurement represents the total amount of protein per serving, including the small amounts from cereals and vegetables.
- The **fat** (g) value reflects the total fat content per serving. Cholesterol values are not given, but they are kept low throughout.
- The **saturated fat** (g) value gives the total saturated fat per serving and includes that found in all animal products, as well as some plant products, e.g. coconut.
- The **fibre** (g) indicates the total quantity of fibre per serving, including soluble and insoluble fibre.
- The **kilojoule** (kJ) value indicates the total energy perserving. To obtain calorie values, simply divide by 4.2.
- The **GL** reflects the glucose load of the serving and represents the impact it will have on blood glucose levels, taking the amount of carbohydrate and the GI into consideration. One serving of any one of the recipes with a GL below 10 will have a minimal impact on blood glucose levels, even if the GI of the dish is intermediate or high. Recipes with higher GL values must be eaten in the recommended serving size to prevent a huge impact on blood glucose levels.
- Although we have not indicated the **sodium** content per serving, we did include it in our analysis, to make sure that most of the recipes have a sodium content of less than 500 mg per serving. There are a few recipes that have a slightly higher sodium content, but this is clearly indicated in the Dieticians' notes of the particular recipe.

  For each recipe, the portions of the different food groups per serving are given. For example, one serving is equivalent to one starch plus one protein. **Consult a dietician if you want to know how many portions of starch, protein, fat, etc., you should consume per day, as this varies according to age, weight, gender, activity, etc. See www.gifoundation.com or www.adsa.org.za to find a dietician in your area.**

  The nutritional contents of one portion for each food group is as follows:

- **Dairy:** the analysis for a low fat dairy portion applies, 530 kJ, 12 g carbohydrate, 8 g protein and 5 g fat.
  Where applicable, the analysis of a fat free dairy portion was used, 340 kJ, 12 g carbohydrate, 8 g protein and 0 g fat.

- **Protein:** the analysis for a medium fat protein portion applies, 328 kJ, 7 g protein and 5.5 g fat.
- **Lean protein:** the analysis for a low fat protein portion applies, 233 kJ, 7 g protein and 3 g fat.
- **Starch:** a starch portion contains 289 kJ, 15 g carbohydrate, 2 g protein and traces of fat.
- **Fat:** a fat portion contains 190 kJ and 5 g fat.
- **Vegetables:** a vegetable portion contains 136 kJ, 6 g carbohydrate and 2 g protein.
- **Fruit:** a fruit portion contains 255 kJ and 15 g carbohydrate.

Measures used

In all the recipes in this book, the following metric measures were used (with abbreviations in brackets):

¼ teaspoon (t)	= 1.25 ml	¼ cup (c)	= 60 ml
½ teaspoon (t)	= 2.5 ml	⅓ cup (c)	= 80 ml
1 teaspoon (t)	= 5 ml	½ cup (c)	= 125 ml
2 teaspoons (t)	= 10 ml etc.	¾ cup (c)	= 185 ml
½ tablespoon (T)	= 7.5 ml	1 cup (c)	= 250 ml
1 tablespoon (T)	= 15 ml	2 cups (c)	= 500 ml
2 tablespoons (T)	= 30 ml etc.	4 cups (c)	= 1 l (litre) etc.

GIFSA's lower fat, GI-rated choice

The GIFSA lower fat, GI-rated choice is indicated by a range of logos that appear on certain products and menus, and show that:

- these products are low(er) in fat, saturated fat, trans fatty acids and cholesterol
- have a GI rating and GL specifications
- allow a minimum of sodium and caffeine
- have fibre specifications.

The Diabetes SA-logo appears on some products in supermarkets. Listed opposite are the logos for the different ratings, with explanations. Please refer to www.gifoundation.com for a glossary of relevant terms.

The recipes in this book are endorsed by GIFSA. GIFSA green plus logo implies that the product: • can be eaten often • is low in total fat (≤ 3 g fat/100 g), low in saturated fat, trans fatty acids and cholesterol • has a very low GI (≤ 40) and GL • has a low sodium and caffeine content • has a high fibre content, where applicable.	
GIFSA green logo implies that the product: • can be eaten often • is lower in total fat (≤ 10 g fat/100 g), saturated fat, trans fatty acids and cholesterol than its regular counterpart • has a low GI (≤ 55) and GL • has a low sodium and caffeine content • has a moderate fibre content, where applicable.	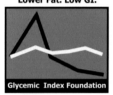
GIFSA orange logo implies that the product: • should be kept for a special treat; people who have diabetes should preferably reserve it for after exercise lasting an hour, or during and after exercise lasting more than one hour • may be slightly higher in total fat, saturated fat, trans fatty acids and cholesterol, but still much lower in fat than its regular counterpart (≤ 15 g fat/100 g) • has an intermediate GI (56–69) and a controlled GL; some of these products could have a low GI, but fall into this group because of a slightly higher fat content • has a moderately low sodium and caffeine content.	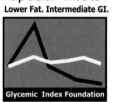
GIFSA red logo implies that the product: • is best for sportsmen and -women after exercise lasting an hour, and during and after exercise lasting more than one hour • is low or moderate in fat, saturated fat, trans fatty acids and cholesterol, but still much lower in fat than its regular counterpart (≤ 15 g fat/100 g) • has a high GI (70+) • has a moderately low sodium and caffeine content.	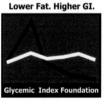
The Diabetes South Africa (DSA) logo is also GI, fat, sodium and caffeine controlled, and is used to indicate that the product is suitable for those with diabetes.	

The Recommended Product List (pages 122–124) contains a list of lower fat, lower GI products available in South Africa. The * just after some food products in the ingredients list of the recipes refers to this list.

GI list of South African lower fat foods

Foods are listed in food groups, in alphabetical order. The GI value of glucose is 100.

Low GI list (GI ≤ 55) Ideal before exercise and when inactive, that is, most of the time						
Dairy	Cereals and porridges	Starches	Fruit	Vegetables	Sugars and Snacks	Drinks
Milk Buttermilk, low fat Low fat and fat free milk (plain and flavoured) **Yoghurt** Low fat and fat free (plain and sweetened) **Custard** Low fat and fat free (unsweetened and sweetened– cooled) **Ice cream** Low fat and fat free (unsweetened and sweetened)	**Cereals** Bokomo Bran Flakes Bokomo Fibre Plus Bokomo Pronutro original with low fat milk Bokomo Pronutro whole wheat (original and apple bake) Kellogg's All Bran Flakes with milk Kellogg's All Bran Fruitful Kellogg's All Bran Hi-Fibre Spar Bran Flakes **Muesli** Bokomo Morning Harvest muesli Fine Form muesli Nature's Source muesli: mixed berries, orange and spices, apple and cinnamon Vital muesli **Porridges** Cooled mealie-meal Jungle oat bran, uncooked Jungle Oats-so-Easy, original Mealtime Instant, original and flavoured Soya Life porridge	**Breads** Dense, heavy loaves Albany low GI brown seed loaf Albany Olde Cape home-style Astoria/Woolworths fruit and honey; sunflower seed whole grain Volkorn rye bread Blue Ribbon brown low GI bread and seed bread Duens seed loaf Fine Form multigrain brown bread Pick 'n Pay whole wheat bread Pumpernickel whole grain rye bread Sasko Confasciano seeded rolls Sasko Daybreaker true whole wheat bread Sasko Nature's Harvest brown seed loaf Sasko soya and linseed bread Sasko Uncle Salie's oats & honey bread Sourdough bread Sunbake fruit and seed loaf Sunbake soya and linseed bread and rolls Woolworths fruit and seed loaf Woolworths low GI seed loaf Woolworths low GI soy lin loaf Woolworths whole grain bread with omega-3 **Crackers** Provita (original and multigrain) **Pasta** All pasta made from durum wheat or durum semolina Fine Form pasta **Legumes** Baked beans Dry beans, peas and lentils, cooked or canned **Rice and other cooked starches** Bulgur wheat Buckwheat Cooled mealie-meal Cooled mealie rice Cooled samp Corn on the cob Pearled barley, whole and cracked Pearled wheat (stampkoring), cooked Spekko Basmati rice, white and brown Spekko brown rice Spekko white rice, long grain, parboiled Tastic rice, white and brown Sweet corn, fresh Sweet potato Whole corn, canned and frozen Wild rice	**Deciduous and berries** Apples, cherries, peaches, pears, plums, strawberries, etc. **Citrus** Grapefruit, naartjies, oranges, lemons, etc. **Other** Prickly pears, kiwi, grapes, mango **Canned fruit** All of the above in fruit juice Pie apples (unsweetened) **Dried fruit** All of the above **Fruit bars** Safari Just Fruit bars TruFruit fruit bars **Fruit juices** Watch portion sizes! Only 125 ml at a time. Apple juice and Appletiser Fresh orange juice Grapetiser, white and red Peartiser Ceres Cloudy Apple and Pear, Passion Fruit, Pineapple, Secrets of the Valley Liquifruit Mango and Orange, Peach and Orange	Most cooked and raw vegetables, including butternut (except those that are intermediate or high GI)	**Sugars** Fructose, not more than 20 g per day Inulin / FOS Isomalt Lactitol Lactose Maltitol Mannitol Polydextrose Sorbitol Sugalite Xylitol **Snacks** Carob (chocolate substitute) Fine Form Green Fig bar Home made low fat popcorn Hummus Instant pudding made with low fat milk Jepsa low GI rusks Just Popcorn Popcorn Affair Lean Buns muffins Nutren Balance bars Prorich diskettes Provita Bites, Cocoa and Oats, Oats and Brown sugar Yotti's low GI Turkish Delight **Jams** Fine Form jam Naturlite fruit spreads	Bioslim nutritional supplement Biozest Bmax Tone-a-Lean D'lightiser Ensure Get-on-Up Get Up & Go Glucerna SR Iced tea lite Mageu Number 1 Milo Mineral water lite Mnandi Amahewu Nutren Active with low fat milk Nutren diabetes/fibre Nutricard Sipahh straws Soya Life drink Sustagen Trophox Tropika da Lite Bokomo Up & Go Vitrace

> For a comprehensive GI and GL list of most foods eaten in South Africa, see *The South African Glycemic Index and Load Guide* by Gabi Steenkamp and Liesbet Delport (GIFSA 2007), available from www.gifoundation.com, www.gabisteenkamp.co.za and most bookstores. Consult your local dietician for help in implementing the GI and GL.

Intermediate GI list (GI 56–69)
Ideal for those with diabetes and sensitive blood sugar, after exercise lasting one hour, or during and after exercise lasting longer than one hour

Dairy	Cereals and porridges	Starches	Fruit	Vegetables	Sugars and Snacks	Drinks
Condensed milk Mega lite ice cream	**Cereals** Bokomo Maximise Bokomo Pronutro Flakes Kellogg's All Bran Flakes Kellogg's All Bran Honey Nut Crunch Kellogg's Coco Pops Crunchers Kellogg's Corn Pops Kellogg's Frosties Kellogg's Strawberry Pops Shredded wheat **Porridges** GI is lowered when cooked in milk Oats: Bokomo, Pick 'n Pay No Name, Spar, Woolworths (cooked and raw) Jungle Oats, cooked Mealie-meal, reheated or with added corn	**Breads** Astoria wheatfree rye breads: pumpkin seed, linseed, pecan nut, mustard and plain Pita bread Sunbake seed loaf Woolworths seed loaf **Crackers** Crackermate lites: sesame and whole wheat Provita, Oats and Brown sugar Ryvita **Cooked Starches** Baby /new potatoes Couscous (durum) Mealie-meal porridge, reheated or with added corn Samp and beans "Sticky" rice (Arborio) Sweet corn, cream-style, canned Tastic Basmati rice	**Tropical fruit** Banana, pawpaw, pineapple, guava, melon **Canned fruit** All fruits canned in syrup **Dried fruit** Sultanas, dates, raisins, currants, cake mix and dried tropical fruit **Fruit juices** Only 125 ml at a time. Most fruit juices, except those listed as high or low GI	Beetroot Marogo Spinach Note: Although some vegetables have an intermediate or high GI, it is not a reason to exclude them from your diet, as most people don't eat large enough portions for the higher GI to have a negative effect on blood glucose levels (one serving of most vegetables has a low GL of less than 5)	**Sugars** Sugar/sucrose **Snacks** Bettasnack home-wheat digestive biscuits Bokomo Quickbreak bran & raisin bar Ouma Nutri rusks Provita Bites, multi-grain **Jams** Jam, homemade Jelly Raw honey	Only 125 ml at a time. Ceres iced tea Regular cold drinks, cordials and soft drinks

High GI list (GI 70+)
Ideal after exercise lasting one hour, or during and after exercise lasting longer than one hour (healthy sportsmen and -women)

Dairy	Cereals and porridges	Starches	Fruit	Vegetables	Sugars and Snacks	Drinks
None	**Cereals** GI is lowered with milk Bokomo Weetbix, regular and sugar free Corn Flakes Kellogg's All Bran toasted muesli Kellogg's Coco Pops Caramel Kellogg's Coco Pops Kellogg's Corn Flakes Crunchy Nut Kellogg's Froot Loops Kellogg's Special K Pronutro, most flavours Puffed wheat Rice Crispies **Porridges** GI is lowered when cooked in milk Instant oats, flavoured Jungle Oats, raw Maltabella Mealie-meal, refined and coarse Morvite Polenta Tiger Oats, raw and cooked	**Breads** All brown, white and ordinary whole wheat bread, all bread rolls and anything made from cake flour, bread flour and Nutty Wheat flour. **Crackers** Corn thins Cream crackers Rice cakes Snackbread, white and whole wheat **Starches** Cake flour Cornflour Gravy powder Jasmine rice Mealie rice Minute noodles Modified starch Pasta made from flour Polenta Potato flour "Regular" potatoes, boiled, mashed, baked, fried, chips Rice flour Samp Soup powder	Litchi Watermelon **Fruit juices** Ceres Litchi and Medley of Fruits **Dried fruit** Dried fruit rolls, sweetened (except apricot)	Green beans with potato Pumpkin (excluding butternut) Turnips and parsnips Although some vegetables have an intermediate or high GI, it is not a reason to exclude them from your diet, as most people do not eat large enough portions for the higher GI to have a negative effect on blood glucose levels (a serving of most vegetables has a low GL of less than 5).	**Sugars** Dextrose Glucose Maltodextrin Maltose **Snacks** Boudoir biscuits Cakes (regular) Marie biscuits Marshmallows Muffins (regular) Scones Sweets, boiled and jelly type Tapioca, boiled with milk Tofu frozen dairy free dessert **Jams** Commercial honey Watermelon preserve	Energade Game Lucozade Powerade

Breakfasts

Muesli muffins
Makes 12 muffins

250 ml flour (1 c)
10 ml baking powder (2 t)
2.5 ml bicarbonate of soda (½ t)
125 ml oat bran* (½ c)
45 ml soft lite margarine*, melted (3 T)
100 ml soft brown sugar **or** Muscovado sugar (⅖ c)
1 egg
1 egg white
80 ml low fat plain yoghurt* (⅓ c)
2 small apples, grated
125 ml muesli*, lower fat, lower GI (½ c)

Nutrients per muffin
GI intermediate (60) • Carbohydrates 23 g
Protein 3 g • Fat 3 g • Saturated fat 1 g
Fibre 2 g • kJ 564 • GL 14
One muffin is equivalent to: 1½ starch + ½ fat

1. Preheat the oven to 190° C.
2. Lightly grease a 12-hole muffin pan, using non-stick cooking spray.
3. Into a large bowl, sift together the flour, baking powder and bicarbonate of soda. Add the oat bran and lift a few times with a spoon to incorporate air.
4. Whisk the margarine, sugar, egg, egg white and yoghurt in a separate bowl.
5. Add the flour mixture to the margarine and sugar mixture, and stir in using a fork. Add the apple and most of the muesli and mix.
6. Spoon into the muffin pan and sprinkle each muffin with the remaining muesli.
7. Bake for 20–25 minutes until cooked through and golden.
8. "Butter" with lower fat cheese spread or low fat cottage cheese and top with lean protein, such as smoked salmon, lean grilled bacon or grated biltong.

Dieticians' notes
- In this recipe we have replaced some of the high GI flour with low GI oat bran and muesli, and were able to reduce the amount of sugar and margarine by adding the apple.
- When apple is added to any batter, the amount of sugar and fat can be reduced.

Apple granola

Serves 6

125 ml flour (½ c)
45 ml soft brown sugar **or** Muscovado sugar (3 T)
60 ml soft lite margarine* (¼ c)
125 ml muesli*, lower fat, lower GI (½ c)
6 small apples
100ml lemon juice (⅖ c)
6 x 100 ml fat free **or** low fat yoghurt

Nutrients per serving
GI low (49) • Carbohydrates 44 g • Protein 6 g
Fat 6 g • Saturated fat 1 g • Fibre 4 g
kJ 1 056 • GL 21
One serving is equivalent to: 1 starch + 1 low fat dairy + 1 fat + 1 fruit

1. Preheat the oven to 200° C and lightly grease a 1–1.5 litre baking dish with non-stick cooking spray.
2. Whizz the flour with the sugar and margarine in a food processor until it resembles breadcrumbs.
3. Stir in the muesli.
4. Peel, core and roughly chop the apples. Toss in lemon juice.
5. Place the apples in the baking dish.
6. Spoon the crumb mixture evenly over the apples and bake for 35 minutes.
7. Divide into six servings and serve each serving with one 100 ml tub of fat free flavoured yoghurt or plain low fat yoghurt, to add protein to the meal.

Dieticians' note
This recipe can also be served as a pudding, as long as the recipe is divided into eight servings instead of six. The GL of such a pudding serving would then be a more suitable 14.

* See page 122 for the recommended product list.

Marinda's French toast treat

Serves 4

This is an unusual way of dressing up French toast.

2 extra large eggs

30 ml water (2 T)

4 rashers back bacon*, lower fat, lower sodium, fat
   removed, chopped

8 mushrooms, sliced

1 clove garlic, chopped, optional

5 ml oil*, canola **or** olive (1 t)

4 slices low GI bread*

30 g lower fat cheese*, grated (size of one matchbox
   before grating)

20 ml sweet chilli sauce (4 t)

Nutrients per serving

GI low (54) • Carbohydrates 22 g • Protein 13 g
Fat 9 g • Saturated fat 3 g • Fibre 3 g
kJ 914 • GL 12
One serving is equivalent to: 1½ starch + 1 protein +
½ fat

---

1. Beat the eggs and water, using a fork.
2. Fry the bacon in a frying pan, which has been sprayed with non-stick cooking spray. Remove from the pan and set aside.
3. Add the mushrooms and garlic to the same pan and stir-fry until the mushrooms are browned. Remove from the pan and set aside.
4. Heat the oil in the same frying pan.
5. Place the bread in a rectangular dish and pour over the egg. Turn so that both sides of all four slices are covered with egg.
6. Fry the egg-covered bread on both sides in the heated oil.
7. Place each slice of French toast on a plate.
8. Sprinkle each slice with a bit of bacon, mushrooms and grated cheese.
9. Grill under a hot grill for a few minutes until the cheese has melted.
10. Evenly drizzle with the sweet chilli sauce.
11. Serve immediately with fresh fruit to make a balanced breakfast.

Sliced baby tomatoes can also be placed on top of the French toast, before the cheese is added.

Dieticians' notes

- Any low GI bread can be used, such as low GI brown, rye or seed loaf bread.
- Although eggs, bacon and cheese (all high fat sources of protein) were used in this dish, each serving contains only one protein and half a fat. This goes to show that you can have eggs, bacon and cheese for breakfast, without the meal being too high in protein and fat, if you control the amounts used.

* See page 122 for the recommended product list.

Riana's breakfast trifle

Serves 4

250 ml muesli*, lower fat, low GI (1 c)

250 ml low fat yoghurt*, vanilla-flavoured **or** plain (1 c)

400 g fruit, such as pawpaw, apple, mango, berries, guava, etc.

250 ml low fat custard*, artificially sweetened (1 c)

Nutrients per serving

GI low (48) • Carbohydrates 46 g • Protein 8 g
Fat 4 g • Saturated fat 1 g • Fibre 5 g
kJ 1 031 • GL 22
One serving is equivalent to: 1 starch + 1 low fat dairy
+ 1 fruit

1. Spoon half of the muesli into a glass bowl or individual dessert glasses.
2. Layer half of the yoghurt, fruit and custard on top of the muesli.
3. Repeat the layers.
4. Refrigerate overnight to soften the muesli, if desired.

If apple or pear is used, drizzle with a bit of lemon juice to prevent discolouration. If banana is used, dip the whole banana with the skin, into boiling water to prevent discolouration.

Dieticians' notes

- Remember that at least half of the fruit you use should be low GI (see the GI list on page 20).
- Note the good fibre content from the low GI, lower fat muesli and the fruit.
- If you like a slightly sweeter breakfast, do not use the plain yoghurt option. However, the GL is the lowest (20) when plain yoghurt is used with low fat, artificially sweetened custard. Usually, we do not recommend the use of artificial sweeteners, but in this case it does help to lower the GL, as this is quite a high carbohydrate meal. Some of the commercially available artificially sweetened custards contain inulin, which is a soluble fibre, and an added bonus.
- The analysis was done using sweetened, low fat vanilla-flavoured yoghurt and low fat, artificially sweetened custard. However, the sugar content per serving is 11 g. This is slightly more than the recommended amount for people with diabetes. Therefore, we recommend that those with diabetes use plain, low fat yoghurt instead of the sweetened vanilla-flavoured yoghurt.
- This is a complete meal. Do not add anything else. However, your usual in-between snack can still be consumed, for example a fruit or a starch portion, or one of the treats from this book.

* See page 122 for the recommended product list.

Caramelised fruit
Serves 4

This is a delicious variation on fruit salad.

4 fresh low GI fruits, such as peach, apple, pear,
  citrus, etc.
160 ml low fat vanilla-flavoured yoghurt* (²⁄₃ c)
160 ml low fat plain yoghurt* (²⁄₃ c)
30 ml soft brown sugar (2 T)

Nutrients per serving
GI low (37) • Carbohydrates 23 g • Protein 4 g
Fat 1.3 g • Saturated fat 0.6 g • Fibre 1 g
kJ 488 • GL 8
One serving is equivalent to: ½ starch + ⅓ low fat
dairy + 1 fruit

1. Remove the pips from the fruit and slice into thick slices.
2. Mix the yoghurts and set aside.
3. Heat a clean frying pan on the stove until hot.
4. Sprinkle the sugar into the hot frying pan and add the fruit.
5. Toss and shake the pan until the sugar is caramelised (2–3 minutes).
6. Serve with 80 ml (⅓ c) of yoghurt per person, and one scrambled egg on one slice of unbuttered toast of your choice.

Two heaped tablespoons of yoghurt are equal to 80 ml (⅓ c).

Dieticians' notes
• The analysis includes half a starch, because of the sugar added to the fruit and in the sweetened yoghurt. We "diluted" the sweetened yoghurt with plain yoghurt, to keep the sugar within limits.
• On its own, this dish is not a complete breakfast. Remember to add one protein and one starch, as we have recommended.

Berry yoghurt
Serves 4

500 ml berries, fresh **or** frozen, such as raspberries,
  blueberries, strawberries (2 c)
125 ml apple juice* (½ c)
10 ml lemon juice (2 t)
45 ml water (3 T)
7.5 ml gelatine (1½ t)
125 ml fresh whole berries (½ c)
250 ml low fat plain yoghurt* (1 c)

Nutrients per serving
GI low (< 30) • Carbohydrates 14 g • Protein 4 g
Fat 1.8 g • Saturated fat 0.6 g • Fibre 3 g
kJ 372 • GL 4
One serving is equivalent to: ½ fruit + ½ low fat dairy

1. Place the 500 ml (2 c) of berries in a saucepan. Lightly crush with a fork, if using frozen berries. Fresh berries may have to be chopped. Add the apple and lemon juice.
2. Simmer for 3 minutes to make a coulis (similar to runny jam). Set aside.
3. Place the water in a cup and sprinkle the gelatine over the water.
4. To dissolve the gelatine, heat the gelatine and water in the microwave on high for 20 seconds, or place the cup with the gelatine and water into a bowl of hot water and stir.
5. Add the warm, dissolved gelatine to the berry coulis and combine.
6. Refrigerate until cold and syrupy.
7. Fold the berry coulis and the fresh berries into the yoghurt to make streaks of fruit through the yoghurt.
8. Spoon the mixture into glasses, and serve with one lower fat, lower GI muffin (page 22 or *Eating for Sustained Energy 1* **and** *2*), topped with a low fat protein.

Dieticians' notes
• We used apple juice to sweeten the berry coulis to reduce the sugar. This gives a deeper flavour and helps to keep the GL much lower. Had we used only sugar to sweeten the berries, the GL would have trebled, as sugar is a highly concentrated source of carbohydrate and should be used only in small amounts – ideally, not more than 10 g (2 t) per meal.
• Note the generous serving size and that it is only equivalent to ½ fruit and ½ dairy. This is because all berries contain very little carbohydrate, and are low GI and therefore low GL as well. In addition, they contain heaps of antioxidants. Even if you double the berry coulis, the GL will still only be 7, which remains acceptable.

* See page 122 for the recommended product list.

Soups

Liesbet's green pea soup
Serves 4

This soup is much quicker and easier to make than
split pea soup.

5 ml oil*, olive **or** canola (1 t)

1 large onion, peeled and chopped

4 rashers back bacon*, lower fat, lower sodium,
   fat removed, chopped

200g baby gem squash (1 punnet)

1 large potato, peeled and cubed

10 ml chicken stock powder* (2 t), dissolved in
   375 ml boiling water (1½ c)

250 ml green peas, fresh, frozen **or** canned, drained (1 c)

1 tin low fat evaporated milk" (380 g)

pinch of nutmeg

black pepper to taste

15 ml fresh parsley, chopped (1 T)

> **Nutrients per serving**
> GI low (45) • Carbohydrates 27 g • Protein 15 g
> Fat 7 g • Saturated fat 2 g • Fibre 5 g
> kJ 1 069 • GL 12
> One serving is equivalent to: 1 starch + 1 low fat dairy
> + 1 lean protein + 1 vegetable

1. Heat the oil in a saucepan and fry the onion until transparent.
2. Add the bacon and stir-fry for another 2 minutes.
3. Top and tail the baby gem squash and cube. Add to the bacon together
   with the potato and prepared chicken stock.
4. Cover and cook on low for 20–30 minutes, or until soft.
5. Add the peas, cover and cook until the peas are heated through.
6. Liquidise all the ingredients and return to the saucepan.
7. Add the milk, nutmeg, black pepper and parsley. Cook over low heat until
   heated through (about 1 minute).
8. Serve with one fruit or a fruit-based pudding, such as the Pear and
   apple envelope (page 112), or the Caramelised fruit (page 28) to make a
   balanced meal that contains enough vegetables and fruit.

Dieticians' notes

• In this recipe, the high GI potato is offset by the low GI green peas and
  evaporated milk.
• Using low fat evaporated milk in soups and sauces is a tasty way to add
  creaminess without the fat of cream.

* See page 122 for the recommended product list.

Sweet corn and sweet potato soup

Makes 4 meal servings or 8 starter servings

10 ml oil*, olive, canola **or** avocado (2 t)

1 large onion, peeled and finely chopped

1 medium sweet potato, peeled, cubed (300 g)

10 ml vegetable stock powder* (2 t)

500 ml water (2 c)

1 bay leaf

pinch of nutmeg

pinch of celery salt

1 ml dried garlic (¼ t)

½ tin creamed sweetcorn (half 410 g tin)

½ tin low fat evaporated milk* (half 380 g tin)

2.5 ml salt (½ t)

freshly ground black pepper

15 ml fresh coriander leaves, chopped (1 T)

15 ml fresh parsley, chopped (1 T)

Nutrients per meal serving
GI low (47) • Carbohydrates 34 g • Protein 7 g
Fat 4 g • Saturated fat 1 g • Fibre 4 g
kJ 880 • GL 16
One meal serving is equivalent to: 1 starch + 1 low fat dairy

---

1. Heat the oil in a large saucepan.
2. Add the onion and cook over medium heat until transparent (about 3 minutes).
3. Add the sweet potato, stock powder, water, bay leaf, nutmeg, celery salt and garlic.
4. Bring to the boil, reduce heat and simmer covered for 30 minutes on low heat, stirring every 5–10 minutes.
5. Once the sweet potatoes are soft, remove the bay leaf and purée the soup.
6. Pour back into the saucepan and add the sweetcorn and the evaporated milk.
7. Season with salt and pepper (and cayenne pepper, if desired).
8. Gently heat through, add the herbs and serve in four soup bowls.
9. Serve with roast vegetables, for example Roast tomato, onion and zucchini (page 84).

This recipe can easily be doubled up if you prefer to use the whole tin of creamed sweet corn and evaporated milk.
Chill in the refrigerator and eat within three days, or freeze until needed.
The orange fleshed sweet potatoes give this soup the lovely rich colour.

Dieticians' notes

- This soup is a meal in itself and no bread should be eaten with it. Fresh fruit for dessert can be served instead of the roast vegetables, to make a balanced meal.
- If half a portion of this soup is eaten as a starter, then slimmers should omit the starch with their next meal.

* See page 122 for the recommended product list.

Cauliflower soup

Makes 4 meal servings or 8 starter servings

750 ml fat free milk* (3 c)

250 ml water (1 c)

2 cloves garlic

1 bunch spring onions

2.5 ml ground cumin (½ t)

5 ml ground turmeric (1 t)

2.5 ml salt (½ t)

black pepper to taste

1 whole cauliflower (about 800 g, 700 g trimmed)

15 ml olive oil* (1 T)

15 ml Parmesan cheese, grated (1 T)

1 slice white bread

2 rashers back bacon*, lower fat, lower sodium, fat
  removed, chopped

Nutrients per meal serving

GI low (38) • Carbohydrates 20 g • Protein 14 g
Fat 6 g • Saturated fat 2 g • Fibre 5 g
kJ 836 • GL 8
One meal serving is equivalent to: 1 low fat dairy
+ 1 lean protein + 1 vegetable

1. Preheat the oven to 200° C.
2. Pour the milk and water into a large saucepan.
3. Peel and roughly chop the garlic, and add to the milk and water mixture.
4. Finely chop the white part of the spring onions and add to the saucepan, keeping the greens for later.
5. Add the cumin, turmeric, salt and pepper.
6. Chop the cauliflower into small pieces and add to the saucepan. Bring to the boil and simmer partially covered for 20 minutes, until the cauliflower is tender.
7. Meanwhile, mix the oil, Parmesan cheese and some pepper in a bowl.
8. Cut the bread into cubes and then coat evenly with the cheese mixture. Spread in a single layer on a baking sheet, and bake for 15–20 minutes, until crisp and brown. Toss at least twice during baking.
9. Fry the chopped bacon over medium heat using non-stick cooking spray. Set aside.
10. Finely slice the spring onion greens and set aside.
11. Purée the soup, either in a food processor or with a hand blender. Add more black pepper if desired and heat through.
12. Ladle into four soup bowls and top with the spring onions, croutons and bacon.
13. Serve with one slice of bread, such as Annekie's health bread (page 52), and a fruit for dessert, to make a balanced meal.

Dieticians' notes

- Unlike all our other recipes in which we use only one teaspoon of oil for four servings, we have used a whole tablespoon of oil in this recipe, as we used fat free or skimmed milk. If low fat milk is used, an extra fat portion per serving will have to be added to the nutritional analysis.
- It is important to use non-stick cooking spray to fry the bacon, as enough oil is already used to crisp and brown the croutons.
- Croutons are generally very high in fat, especially if served with bacon and Parmesan cheese (both also high in fat, particularly saturated fat). In this recipe, however, we used lean bacon, just enough Parmesan to give flavour, and a controlled amount of oil.
- This soup can also be served as a starter for eight people. One serving would then be equivalent to one lean protein and ½ vegetable.

* See page 122 for the recommended product list.

John's roast vegetable soup
Serves 8

This is a lovely, different way of serving roast vegetables.

5 fresh ripe tomatoes, quartered

1 large brinjal, cubed (300 g)

2 large red peppers, cored and cut into 2 cm squares

250 g patty pans, halved or quartered depending on size (1 punnet)

1 medium sweet potato, peeled and cut into 2 cm cubes (300 g)

2 large onions, peeled and quartered

15 ml oil*, olive **or** canola (1 T)

1.25 ml salt (¼ t)

20 ml vegetable stock powder* (4 t), dissolved in 1.5 litre water (6 c)

5 ml dried thyme (1 t) **or** 15 ml fresh thyme (1 T)

2.5 ml dried oregano (½ t) **or** 7.5 ml fresh oregano (½ T)

5 ml dried basil (1 t) **or** 15 ml fresh basil (1 T)

1.25 ml salt (¼ t)

1.25 ml freshly ground black pepper (¼ t)

Nutrients per meal serving
GI low (36) • Carbohydrates 19 g • Protein 3 g
Fat 2 g • Saturated fat 0.3 g • Fibre 5 g
kJ 500 • GL 7
One serving is equivalent to: ½ starch + ½ fat + 2 vegetables

1. Preheat the oven to 200° C.
2. Place all the vegetables in a large bowl and coat with the oil, 1.25ml (¼ t) salt and a little black pepper.
3. Pour into a roasting pan and cover with foil, shiny side down.
4. Place in the oven and turn the temperature down to 180° C. Roast covered for 20 minutes, and then uncovered for another 15 minutes until most of the vegetables have a nice roasted look.
5. Spoon into a large saucepan with the prepared stock, herbs, salt and pepper. Bring to the boil and simmer covered, for 20 minutes.
6. Remove from the heat and purée, or keep the vegetables chunky if you prefer. Return to the stove and reheat.
7. Serve with a slice of bread of your choice, topped with cheese (one matchbox per slice), melted in the microwave for 20–30 seconds on high, if desired.

Variation
Slice the top off two heads of garlic to expose all the cloves and add to the vegetables in the roasting pan. Remove before puréeing and spread onto the bread, if desired.

Sweet potato is inclined to discolour once it has been peeled and cut. Therefore, place it under water immediately, until ready for use.

Dieticians' notes
- Do not butter the bread if regular cheese is used, as the soup and cheese already make up about 10 g of fat and the ideal meal should contain no more than 13 g of fat.
- Note the high fibre content from all the vegetables.

* See page 122 for the recommended product list.

Salads

Layered salad
Serves 4

This is a deliciously different way of serving a mixed salad – even those who do not like lettuce will enjoy this salad.

250 ml green peas, fresh **or** frozen (1 c)

1 small onion, peeled and halved

2 rashers back bacon*, lower fat, lower sodium, fat removed **or** 1 slice smoked ham (60 g)

60 ml lower fat mayonnaise* (¼ c)

30 ml low fat **or** fat free milk* (2 T)

250 g lettuce **or** baby spinach, thinly sliced (one packet or half a medium lettuce head)

½ English cucumber, quartered lengthwise and thinly sliced, optional

90 g fat reduced Feta cheese*, crumbled (1 round)

5 ml sugar (1 t)

freshly ground black pepper

Nutrients per serving

GI low (35) • Carbohydrates 10 g • Protein 9 g
Fat 8 g • Saturated fat 4 g • Fibre 4 g
kJ 687 • GL 3
One serving is equivalent to: 1 protein + ½ fat
+ 2 vegetables

---

1. Pour boiling water over the peas, drain and set aside.
2. Cut the onion halves into thin slices and pour boiling water over them. Drain and set aside.
3. Dice the bacon or ham and fry until browned, using non-stick cooking spray on the pan.
4. Mix the mayonnaise and milk in a cup. Add a little extra milk, if the dressing is too thick.
5. Take a deep glass bowl or dish of 150–200 mm diameter and layer the salad, starting with lettuce, followed by peas, onion, bacon, cucumber, Feta cheese, black pepper, sugar and lastly the mayonnaise mixture.
6. Repeat the layers two or three times.
7. Serve immediately.

Dieticians' notes

- As one serving of this salad contains one portion of protein (provided by the bacon and Feta) and half a portion of fat, be sure to eat less protein when serving this salad.
- This salad can also be served as a light meal, together with a slice of lower GI bread.
- Do not stress about the sugar in this salad. It is only 0.7 g per serving and has no effect on the GI.
- If you choose to use black pepper or herbed Feta cheese, remember that the fat content will be higher, as these flavour variants do not come in the lower fat version.

* See page 122 for the recommended product list.

Continental cucumber and dill salad
Serves 4

This is a delicious salad to make ahead of time to serve with any quick lunch of lean cold meats and salads.

1 English cucumber, halved lengthwise and thinly sliced (500 g)
5 ml salt (1 t)
1 small onion, peeled, very finely chopped
10 ml sugar (2 t)
1 ml salt (¼ t)
1 ml freshly ground black pepper (¼ t)
30 ml fresh dill, finely chopped (2 T) **or** 5 ml dried dill (1 t)
30 ml white grape vinegar (2 T)
125 ml fat free plain yoghurt* (½ c)
30 ml fat reduced cream* (2 T), optional

Nutrients per serving
GI low (<30) • Carbohydrates 9 g • Protein 3 g
Fat 1.8 g • Saturated fat 1.2 g • Fibre 2 g
kJ 292 • GL 3
One serving is equivalent to: 1 vegetable + ⅓ low fat dairy

1. Spread the cucumber slices onto a dinner plate and sprinkle the salt evenly over the slices. Make sure all the slices are salted by turning the slices over a little.
2. Leave for about an hour, so that the cucumber slices become limp.
3. Meanwhile, place the onion in a medium bowl and sprinkle with the sugar, salt, pepper and dill. Stir and then leave to stand, so that the onion can sweat. This draws out the "bite" from the onion.
4. Add the vinegar to the onion mixture, as well as the yoghurt and the cream, and mix to make the dressing.
5. Remove handfuls of cucumber slices from the plate and gently squeeze out all the excess liquid. Add to the dressing and mix well, making sure every slice is well covered with dressing.
6. Store in a covered glass bowl in the fridge until needed.
7. Serve as one of the vegetables at any meal.

This salad keeps for 10 days in the fridge if stored in a covered glass bowl. Use fresh dill as it always tastes much better than the dried herb.

Dieticians' notes
• Most of the first lot of salt is discarded with the juices that are squeezed out of the cucumber. This means that the salad remains well within the sodium recommendations.
• The small amount of sugar in this recipe (2 g per person) is offset by the large amount of cucumber and the yoghurt.
• Remember to use the fat-reduced cream (12–21% fat), rather than whipping cream (37% fat), as cream contains mainly saturated fats that increase the risk for heart disease. The small amount of cream in this recipe is acceptable, even though it is mainly saturated fat.
• Although one serving of this salad is equivalent to one veg and some dairy, it can be regarded as just a vegetable.

* See page 122 for the recommended product list.

Hildegard's potato salad
Serves 10

1 kg unblemished baby potatoes, washed
1 small onion, peeled
1 clove garlic, peeled
15 ml fresh rosemary leaves (1 T)
15 ml fresh parsley, chopped (1 T)
125 g low fat **or** fat free smooth cottage cheese* (½ tub)
80 ml low fat **or** fat free plain yoghurt* (⅓ c)
80 ml low oil mayonnaise* (⅓ c)
125 ml hot water (½ c)
5 ml vegetable stock powder* (1 t)
30 ml white wine vinegar (2T), optional
freshly ground black pepper
3 large hard-boiled eggs

Nutrients per serving
GI low (54) • Carbohydrates 24 g • Protein 6 g
Fat 5 g • Saturated fat 1.2 g • Fibre 2 g
kJ 692 • GL 13
One serving (½ c) is equivalent to: 1 starch + ½ dairy + ½ fat

1. Boil the baby potatoes until soft.
2. Pour off the hot water and leave to cool for an hour.
3. Cut the cold baby potatoes in half, or if they are bigger, into bite-sized chunks. It is usually not necessary to peel baby potatoes unless the skin is blemished, in which case it is more appetising to peel them.
4. Place the onion, garlic, rosemary, parsley, cottage cheese, yoghurt and mayonnaise into a blender and whizz until the onion is finely chopped.
5. Pour the hot water over the stock powder in a cup, and add to the dressing in the blender. Blend to make a fairly runny dressing.
6. Add the vinegar, if desired.
7. Pour the dressing over the potato chunks and gently combine.
8. Season with the pepper to taste.
9. Chill for at least 2 hours.
10. Just before serving, peel the hard-boiled eggs and chop roughly.
11. Add to the potato salad and gently mix through or pile on top, as preferred.
12. Serve 125 ml (½ c) of this salad as the starch at any meal.

Variation
Add some finely chopped red pepper or fresh chilli, or chopped Peppadews, if you prefer a more tangy potato salad.

Dieticians' notes
• Baby potatoes are absorbed more slowly than regular potatoes, making them a better choice for potato salad. Leaving the skins on adds not only brown colour to the otherwise white and green salad, but also a little fibre.
• The dressing for this salad is made without the traditional high fat mayonnaise, making it much lower in fat.
• Adding hard-boiled eggs to a potato salad adds depth of flavour. The cholesterol in the eggs (divided into 10 portions) is of little consequence, even for those with a cholesterol problem, as it is so little. It is the saturated fat in steak or chops traditionally eaten with potato salad that will increase the risk for heart disease.
• Potatoes are a dense source of carbohydrate and should thus be eaten in small amounts. Make sure you stick to the small, recommended serving. A man's serving would be one and a half times this serving size.

* See page 122 for the recommended product list.

Tangy tossed salad
Serves 4

This is a deliciously different tossed salad with ingredients such as cottage cheese with Feta, Peppadews and apples.

½ small onion, quartered and thinly sliced, optional
1 packet mixed lettuce, shredded (100 g)
2 small red apples, sliced and sprinkled with lemon juice
¼ English cucumber, sliced and halved
4 Peppadews, thinly sliced
125 ml low fat chunky cottage cheese with Feta* (1:1 mix), drained (½ c)
freshly ground black pepper

1. Blanch the onion in a little boiling water, if desired.
2. Mix all the ingredients in a large salad bowl.
3. Serve with a lower GI starch and lower fat protein to make a balanced meal.

The chunky cottage cheese with Feta is a ready-made product. If you cannot find it, use herbed, low fat, chunky cottage cheese, mixed with fat reduced Feta in a 1:1 ratio to make up 125 ml (½ c).

Dieticians' note
The sugar in the Peppadews is so little that it will not raise the GI. In addition, all the other ingredients are also low GI.

Nutrients per serving
GI low (35) • Carbohydrates 14 g • Protein 6 g
Fat 4 g • Saturated fat 1 g • Fibre 2 g
kJ 493 • GL 5
One serving is equivalent to: ½ protein + 2 vegetables

Spinach, chickpea and sun-dried tomato salad
Serves 6

1 packet sun-dried tomatoes (60 g)
½ packet baby spinach (125 g)
45 ml fresh sweet basil, chopped (3 T)
1 tin chickpeas*, drained (410 g)
15 ml olive oil* (1 T)
30 ml balsamic vinegar (2 T)
30 ml lemon juice, preferably freshly squeezed (2 T)
10 ml mustard powder (2 t)
5 ml sugar (1 t)
freshly ground black pepper
1 round fat reduced Feta cheese*, cubed (about 90 g)

1. Place the tomatoes in boiling water for 1 minute.
2. Arrange the spinach, basil and drained chickpeas on a serving dish and add the tomatoes.
3. For the dressing, mix the olive oil, balsamic vinegar, lemon juice, mustard powder and sugar, and pour over the salad.
4. Add black pepper to taste and toss the salad.
5. Add the cheese to the salad.

The taste of the salad can be varied by using black pepper or herbed Feta cheese, but then the fat will be higher, as these variants of Feta are not available in the fat reduced variety.

Dieticians' notes
• Sun-dried tomatoes that have been preserved in olive oil may improve the taste of the salad, but the fat content will also be higher.
• This is a good example of how higher GI spinach is still acceptable, even in a salad, because the GL of spinach is low.
• This salad is suitable as a light meal.

* See page 122 for the recommended product list.

Nutrients per serving
GI low (< 30) • Carbohydrates 17 g • Protein 8 g
Fat 7 g • Saturated fat 2.7 g • Fibre 4g
kJ 713 • GL 4
One serving is equivalent to: ½ starch + 1 protein + ½ fat + 1 vegetable

Mixed salad with peaches and vinaigrette

Serves 4

1 tin peaches (825 g) **or** 4 fresh peaches or nectarines,
  halved or sliced
100 g selection of greens, such as lettuce, baby spinach,
  rocket, basil, etc.
12 cherry tomatoes, halved
4 baby spring onions, chopped
freshly ground black pepper
30 ml lemon juice (2 T), optional
2 cloves garlic, crushed
60 ml balsamic vinegar, brown or white (4 T)
20 ml oil*, olive **or** avocado (4 t)
5 ml sugar (1 t) **or** 10 ml peach syrup (2 t)
10 ml fresh herbs (2 t) **or** 5 ml dried herbs (1 t), such as
  parsley, thyme, basil, etc.
2.5 ml celery salt (½ t)
30 ml water (2 T)

Nutrients per serving
GI low (36) • Carbohydrates 16 g • Protein 1 g
Fat 5 g • Saturated fat 0.6 g • Fibre 2g
kJ 479 • GL 6
One serving is equivalent to: 1 fruit + 1 fat

1. Spray a griddle pan with non-stick cooking spray. Fry the fruit in the pan for 2 minutes on high on each side until they start to soften, and show decorative black lines.
2. Place the greens, tomatoes and spring onions on a serving platter or on four plates. Add cucumber and sweet pepper, if desired.
3. Place the peaches or nectarines on top. Add freshly ground black pepper.
4. In a serving jug, make the vinaigrette by mixing the lemon juice, garlic, vinegar, oil, sugar (or peach syrup), fresh herbs, celery salt and water.
5. Serve the salad with the vinaigrette on the side as one of the vegetables of a meal.

A vinaigrette is normally made with two parts oil and one part vinegar. In this recipe, we have used one part oil and six parts vinegar, and diluted it with water, without sacrificing flavour.

Dieticians' note

Although this salad contains one fat per serving, it is all from the olive oil in the dressing, which is an excellent source of mono-unsaturated fatty acids (MUFAs). One third of our fat intake should come from such a source. Replacing saturated fats in your diet with MUFAs increases insulin sensitivity and thereby protects against diabetes. MUFAs also reduce the risk for heart and vascular (blood vessel) diseases.

John's warm tomato salad

Serves 4

A warm salad is a welcome change from the usual tomato and onion salad.

125 ml balsamic vinegar (½ c)
15 ml soft brown sugar (1 T)
1.25 ml salt (¼ t)
10 ml olive oil* (2 t)
500 g cherry tomatoes
1.25 ml freshly ground black pepper (¼ t)

Nutrients per serving
GI low (30) • Carbohydrates 7 g • Protein 1 g
Fat 3 g • Saturated fat 0.4 g • Fibre 2 g
kJ 244 • GL 2
One serving is equivalent to: 1 vegetable + ½ fat

1. Pour the balsamic vinegar, brown sugar and salt into a frying pan or shallow saucepan.
2. On low to medium heat, reduce the vinegar until it is thick and syrupy (about 5 minutes). Be careful not to burn the syrup.
3. Add the oil.
4. Add the cherry tomatoes and turn up the heat to medium high. The tomatoes will start to split, releasing some of their juice into the syrup. The syrup will start to thin out a little.
5. Keep stirring or tossing the tomatoes in the syrup until they are all coated and show signs of splitting. Season with the pepper.
6. Serve as one of the vegetables at any meal.

Dieticians' note

Lycopene is particularly good for protection against prostate cancer, so be sure to serve tomatoes to the man in your life as often as possible. Lycopene is more bio-available in cooked tomatoes than in raw tomatoes.

* See page 122 for the recommended product list.

Light meals

Tropical toastie
Serves 4

This is a delicious variation of bread and cheese – quick and easy to make.

4 slices low GI bread*
4 rashers back bacon* (lower fat, lower sodium), fat removed and chopped
30 ml chutney (2 T)
2 medium bananas, peeled and sliced **or** 4 thin rings of pineapple
15 ml fresh thyme, chopped (1 T) **or** 5 ml dried thyme (1 t)
60 g lower fat cheese*, grated (size of two matchboxes before grating)

Nutrients per serving
GI low (55) • Carbohydrates 30 g • Protein 11 g
Fat 7 g • Saturated fat 2 g • kJ 976
Fibre 3 g • GL 17
One serving is equivalent to: 1 starch + 1½ protein + ⅔ fruit

1. Preheat the oven to 180° C.
2. Toast the bread and place on a lightly greased baking sheet.
3. Cook the bacon in a frying pan that has been sprayed with non-stick cooking spray, or in the microwave until done. Set aside.
4. Spread the chutney evenly over the four slices of toast.
5. Place the banana or pineapple slices evenly on the toast. Sprinkle the bacon on top.
6. Sprinkle the thyme and cheese on the fruit and bacon, dividing evenly between the four slices of toast.
7. Bake for 4–6 minutes.
8. Serve with a salad or vegetable soup.

Dieticians' note
- Any lean bacon with the fat removed can be used. However, people with high blood pressure should use the lower sodium version.
- As this meal does not contain a fat portion, you can either fry the bacon in a little extra virgin olive oil or spread each slice with 15 ml (1 T) of mashed avocado before adding the fruit. Alternatively, you may choose to have one tablespoon of nuts mixed with one tablespoon of sultanas or raisins as dessert or an in-between snack. Olive oil, most nuts and avocado are good sources of the more beneficial mono-unsaturated fats.

Lowveld avo snacker
Serves 4

4 slices low GI bread*
100 g avocado (½ medium)
1.25 ml salt (¼ t)
freshly ground black pepper
120 g lower fat cheese*, grated (size of four matchboxes before grating)
30 ml sweet chilli sauce (2 T)

Nutrients per serving
GI low (52) • Carbohydrates 21 g • Protein 14 g
Fat 13 g • Saturated fat 4 g • Fibre 3g
kJ 1 077 • GL 11
One serving is equivalent to: 1½ starch + 1½ protein + 1 fat

1. Preheat the oven to 180° C.
2. Toast the bread lightly in a toaster.
3. Place the toast on a lightly greased baking sheet.
4. Mash the avocado and flavour with a little salt and pepper. Spread evenly on the slices of toast.
5. Divide the cheese between the slices of toast to cover the avocado.
6. Place in the oven and bake for 3–5 minutes.
7. Drizzle the sweet chilli sauce over the avo snackers.
8. Serve immediately with baby tomatoes, cucumber fingers, snap peas and butter lettuce drizzled with balsamic vinegar, but no oil.

Dieticians' note
- This is an example of how margarine, which is high in poly-unsaturated fatty acids, can be replaced with avocado, which is high in mono-unsaturated fatty acids. Remember that the most natural fat to the body is mono-unsaturated.
- The total fat of this meal is already at the recommended level of 13 g per meal so it is better not to add another fat (no oil in the dressing on the salad).
- Sweet chilli sauce is thickened with corn flour and is high in sugar, making it a concentrated source of carbohydrate, and thus has a high GL and GI. This also applies to many other condiments. All sauces and condiments should thus be used in small amounts.

* See page 122 for the recommended product list.

Smoked chicken salad
Serves 4

Red apples look particularly attractive in this lovely summer lunch.

12 small baby potatoes, quartered
1 large apple, cored and sliced
15 ml fresh lemon juice (1 T)
1 packet assorted lettuce leaves, torn into pieces (100 g)
2 smoked chicken breasts, sliced (220g)
30 ml cashew nuts (2 T) **or** 10 pecan nut halves
1 bunch chives, chopped (10 g)
60 ml fat reduced mayonnaise* (¼ c)
60 ml fat free or low fat milk* **or** yoghurt* (¼ c)
freshly ground black pepper

Nutrients per serving including starch
GI low (61) • Carbohydrate 27 g • Protein 20 g
Fat 7 g • Saturated fat 1.4 g • Fibre 3 g
kJ 1 065 • GL 14
One serving is equivalent to: 2 lean protein +
1½ starch + ½ fat + ⅓ fruit

1. Cook the baby potatoes while preparing the rest of the salad.
2. In a flat dish, cover the sliced apples with the lemon juice to prevent discolouration.
3. In a salad bowl or platter, arrange the lettuce leaves, chicken and apple slices.
4. Add the baby potatoes (they can still be warm) and toss lightly.
5. Sprinkle the nuts and chives on top.
6. Mix the mayonnaise and milk or yoghurt to form a thick sauce and serve with the chicken salad.

It is not necessary to peel the apple, unless you or one of your guests suffers from irritable bowel syndrome (IBS).
If you prefer a thinner dressing, use milk instead of yoghurt with the mayonnaise.
Instead of the baby potatoes as the starch, one slice of low GI bread or three to four low GI crackers per person can be used.

Variation
Replace the apple with another fruit, such as peach, pear, etc.

Dieticians' notes
- Nuts always add depth of flavour to chicken salad, but they are high in fat (although beneficial) and thus the portion needs to be controlled.
- Remember that smoked chicken is quite high in sodium, so if you suffer from high blood pressure, it would be better to use regular cooked chicken

* See page 122 for the recommended product list.

Annekie's health bread

Makes two loaves – cut into 16 slices each

500 ml fat free milk*, lukewarm (2 c)

15 ml raw honey **or** molasses (1 T)

10 ml bicarbonate of soda (2 t)

750 ml bread **or** cake flour (3 c)

5 ml salt (1 t)

10 ml baking powder (2 t)

250 ml lower GI oats* (1 c)

250 ml oat bran* (1 c)

500 ml digestive bran (2 c)

15 ml chopped nuts, any kind (1 T)

15 ml sunflower seeds (1 T)

15 ml sesame seeds (1 T)

15 ml linseeds (1 T)

15 ml poppy seeds (1 T)

15 ml brown sugar (1 T)

250 ml sultanas (1 c)

2 medium apples, peeled and grated

1 large carrot, peeled and grated

60 ml oil*, canola **or** any nut oil (4 T)

Nutrients per slice

GI intermediate (60) • Carbohydrates 21 g
Protein 3 g • Fat 3 g • Saturated fat 0.4 g
Fibre 3 g • kJ 548 • GL 13
One slice is equivalent to: 1½ starch + ½ fat

---

1. Mix the milk, honey and bicarb in a medium bowl or jug and leave to foam slightly. Set aside.
2. Preheat the oven to 180° C and spray two 220 x 120 mm loaf pans with non-stick cooking spray.
3. Sift the flour, salt and baking powder into a large mixing bowl. Add the rest of the dry ingredients, excluding the fruit and carrot, and lift up a few times with a spoon to incorporate air.
4. Add the sultanas, grated apples, carrot, oil and the milk mixture. Mix well.
5. Spoon into the prepared loaf pans and bake for about 45 minutes until a skewer inserted into the centre of each loaf comes out clean.
6. Remove from the oven and cool for 30 minutes on a cooling rack before removing the loaves from the bread pans.
7. Slice into 16 slices per loaf, and serve one slice as the starch of any meal.

This bread freezes well for up to three months. Freeze it sliced, and defrost each slice in a toaster as required.

Dieticians' notes

- The apple and carrot not only add moisture and colour, but also help to lower the GI of this health bread.
- This is the perfect bread for open sandwiches and for using in the Lowveld avo snacker recipe (page 48).
- The light meal example shown alongside contains only 1 matchbox of lean protein per person – shaved ham, shaved cheese and low fat cottage cheese – together with generous amounts of vegetables and/or fruit.

* See page 122 for the recommended product list.

An update on seeds

The 30% of fat found in most seeds is predominantly in the form of poly-unsaturated fatty acids (PUFAs). In contrast to this, the 50% of fat in most nuts is predominantly in the form of mono-unsaturated fatty acids (MUFAs).

However, the PUFAs in linseeds (linoleic acid or LA) are mostly in the form of omega-3, whereas the PUFAs in other seeds are mostly omega-6. Keep in mind that fish omega-3 sources (EPA and DHA) are superior to those from plants and therefore we all should try to eat fatty fish at least once, but preferably twice a week.

Marina's ostrich carpaccio

Serves 4 or 8 starter portions

250 g ostrich fillet* (½ packet)

45 ml lemon juice, preferably fresh (3 T)

2 cloves garlic, chopped finely

freshly ground black pepper

10 ml avocado oil (2 t)

12–16 rocket leaves

10 ml Parmesan **or** Pecorino cheese, shaved or
   finely grated (2 t)

4 slices low GI bread*, optional

Nutrients per serving including the bread

GI low (51) • Carbohydrates 15 g • Protein 19 g
Fat 6 g • Saturated fat 0.8 g • Fibre 2 g
kJ 755 • GL 8
One serving is equivalent to: 2 lean protein + 1 starch

1. Remove the ostrich fillets from the packet and place half of them separately onto a plastic plate. Freeze for about 2 hours to make slicing much easier.
2. Remove from the freezer – the fillets will be semi-frozen – and slice as thinly as possible.
3. Place the ostrich slices into a glass container and cover with the lemon juice, garlic, plenty of black pepper and oil. Marinate, covered for 20–30 minutes.
4. Divide the rocket leaves onto four plates.
5. Layer the ostrich slices evenly onto the leaves.
6. Top with two curls of shaved Parmesan or Pecorino.
7. Cut each slice of bread into three fingers and serve with the carpaccio.
8. Serve with a large mixed salad or fruit salad for dessert.

The remaining half packet of ostrich fillet can be dry fried and kept for lunch the next day. Combine with a large tossed salad and serve with low GI crackers or bread.

Dieticians' notes

- Fresh lemon juice significantly enhances the flavour of the carpaccio. Acidic foods, such as lemon juice, slow the emptying of the stomach and thus lower the GI of meals. Be liberal in the use of lemon juice.
- Do not spread the bread with margarine or butter, but rather use it to mop up the marinade.
- If serving this as a starter, use half the bread (one bread finger per serving). This serving would then be equivalent to one lean protein plus half a starch.
- Ostrich is very low in fat (0.4 g of fat per 100 g, or truly fat free) and therefore ideal for meat dishes. Also try ostrich mince as a fat free alternative to regular mince. Even replacing half of the mince with ostrich mince will reduce the fat content significantly.
- Parmesan cheese, like most regular cheeses, is very high in fat and saturated fats. However, it is usually used just to add flavour. The small portion used in this recipe is completely adequate.
- To make a balanced light meal, it is important to serve only one slice of bread per person with the carpaccio. Add a salad or some roast vegetables, or add a fruit, to make up your antioxidant quota in this meal.

* See page 122 for the recommended product list.

Chicken dishes

Tangy chicken bake
Serves 4

To shorten the cooking time, precook the chicken and the pasta.

4 skinned chicken breasts **or** 440 g cooked chicken

2.5 ml garlic flakes (½ t) **or** 1 clove garlic

2.5 ml mixed herbs (½ t)

125 g shell noodles*, durum wheat (¼ of 500 g packet)

500 ml boiling water (2 c)

60 ml low fat mayonnaise (¼ c)

60 ml chutney, preferably lite (¼ c)

60 ml tomato sauce, preferably lite (¼ c)

⅓ packet onion soup powder (15 g or 2 T)

250 g mushrooms, sliced (1 punnet) **or** 1 tin mushrooms, drained (410 g)

Nutrients per serving
GI low (48) • Carbohydrates 35 g • Protein 38 g
Fat 7 g • Saturated fat 1.5 g • Fibre 3 g
kJ 1 549 • GL 17
One serving is equivalent to: 4 lean protein + 2 starch
+ ½ vegetable

---

1. Flavour the chicken with the garlic and herbs and cook in 200 ml (⅖ c) of water for 30 minutes, or in the microwave, covered, on medium for 10 minutes. Alternatively, use cooked leftover chicken.
2. Preheat the oven to 160° C.
3. Boil the noodles in the boiling water with a pinch of salt until al dente.
4. Mix the mayonnaise, chutney, tomato sauce and soup powder in a cup. Add water to fill the cup to 250 ml and mix well. Set aside.
5. Cube the chicken and combine with the noodles, mushrooms and sauce in an ovenproof dish, and bake uncovered for 30 minutes until bubbling. After 15 minutes, stir the bake and check that there is still enough gravy – if not, add another 75 ml (5 T) of water. Stir in and bake for the remaining 15 minutes.
6. Serve with lots of mixed vegetables, a large salad or a fruit pudding, such as Spicy poached pears (page 100) or Caramelised fruit (page 28), as this dish does not contain enough vegetables or fruit.

Dieticians' notes

- As the fat content of this meal is just over half of the 13 g of fat recommended for a meal, chicken thighs and drumsticks (one of each per person, skinned before cooking) can be used instead of the leaner chicken breasts. As soon as chicken breasts are used, the protein content of the meal can easily be exceeded, as white chicken meat is a highly concentrated source of protein.
- Remember that packet soups, tomato sauce and chutney are all high in sodium, which should be eaten in moderation by all those suffering from high blood pressure. Make sure you have no other high sodium (salt) foods on the day that you eat this dish. Alternatively, you could replace half of the soup powder with 30 ml (2 T) of oat bran, as the soup powder has the highest sodium content.
- It is better to use lite tomato sauce and chutney in this recipe as they are a less concentrated source of carbohydrate (no sugar). This will save you half a starch portion per serving. The analysis shown is for regular tomato sauce and chutney.
- Adding half a plate of vegetables to any meal adds about 5 GL. So adding the half plate of vegetables to this dish with a GL of 17 brings the total GL for the meal to 22, which is acceptable for a main meal.
- When buying pasta, check on the ingredients list that it is made from durum wheat, as the GI of such pasta is lower than pasta made from flour, including homemade pasta.

* See page 122 for the recommended product list.

Fruity chicken curry
Serves 4

This is a quick and easy dish.

185 ml rice* (¾ c)
5 ml oil*, olive **or** canola (1 t)
4 chicken thighs, skinned
4 chicken drumsticks, skinned
2 medium onions, peeled and thinly sliced
1 clove garlic, peeled and crushed
1 apple, chopped
30 ml lower GI oats* (2 T)
10–20 ml curry powder (2–4 t)
2.5 ml ground ginger (½ t)
2.5 ml ground cinnamon (½ t)
10 ml chicken stock powder* (2 t), dissolved in
  250 ml boiling water (1 c)
30 ml chutney (2 T)
250 g mushrooms, sliced (1 punnet), optional
15 ml tomato paste **or** sauce (1 T)
freshly ground black pepper
1 banana
2 peach halves (canned in juice), drained **or**
  1 fresh peach, chopped
60 g pineapple, cubed (1 slice)
30 ml lemon juice (2 T)

Nutrients per serving with rice
GI low (43) • Carbohydrates 44 g • Protein 33 g
Fat 12 g • Saturated fat 3 g • Fibre 4 g
kJ 1 810 • GL 19
One serving is equivalent to: 4 protein + 2 starch
+ 1 fruit

1. Cook the rice in lightly salted water until just tender.
2. Heat the oil in a large frying pan and fry the chicken pieces on both sides until brown. Set aside.
3. Add the onion, garlic and apple, and fry until soft.
4. Sprinkle oats, curry powder, ginger and cinnamon over, and stir-fry for 1 minute to develop the flavour.
5. Add the prepared chicken stock slowly and bring to the boil.
6. When the sauce has thickened, add the chutney, (mushrooms) and tomato paste or sauce, and season to taste with the pepper.
7. Put the chicken pieces back into the frying pan, reduce the heat, cover and allow to simmer for 20–30 minutes until the chicken is cooked.
8. Peel and slice the banana. Add the banana, peach, pineapple, and lemon juice to the chicken and heat thoroughly.
9. Serve with the rice and a large tossed salad.

Dieticians' notes

- In this recipe we have used oats instead of flour or cornflour to thicken the dish. It is just as effective and, as well as yielding a lower GI end product, more filling.
- Adding half a plate of salad to any meal adds from 1 – 2 GL. So adding the half plate of vegetable salad to this dish with a GL of 19 brings the total GL to 20 or 21 – ideal for a main meal.

* See page 122 for the recommended product list.

Korma chicken with crushed sweet potato

Serves 4

5 ml oil*, canola **or** olive (1 t)

4 chicken breasts, deboned and skinned

1 large onion, finely chopped

10 ml fresh garlic, crushed (2 t)

5 ml curry **or** masala powder (1 t)

2.5 ml turmeric (½ t)

pinch ground cloves

pinch ground cinnamon

pinch ground ginger

1.25 ml cumin seeds (¼ t) **or** 2.5 ml ground cumin (½ t)

1 bay leaf

1.25 ml celery salt (¼ t)

2.5 ml salt (½ t)

250 ml water (1 c)

30 ml fresh lemon juice (2 T)

30 ml chutney (2 T) **or** 15 ml apricot jam (1 T)

1 bunch fresh coriander leaves, roughly chopped (30g)

1 large sweet potato, cooked (500 g)

Nutrients per serving
GI low (48) • Carbohydrates 32 g • Protein 35 g
Fat 6 g • Saturated fat 1.5 g • Fibre 5 g
kJ 1 424 • GL 15
One serving is equivalent to: 4 lean protein
+ 1½ starch + 1 vegetable

1. Heat the oil in a non-stick saucepan, add the cubed chicken and brown on high heat, stirring all the time. Remove from the saucepan and set aside.
2. Add the onion to the same saucepan and fry gently on medium heat until transparent.
3. Add the garlic and spices, and cook over medium heat, stirring all the time to develop the flavour.
4. Add the water, lemon juice, chutney or apricot jam. Simmer for 5 minutes.
5. Add the cubed chicken pieces and simmer covered, for 20–30 minutes.
6. Stir in the fresh coriander leaves and spoon into a baking dish, reserving some of the gravy to add to the sweet potato.
7. Using a fork, roughly mash the sweet potato with the reserved gravy, just enough to give a slightly lumpy mash.
8. Pile the crushed sweet potato on top of the chicken in the casserole dish.
9. Brown under a hot grill, and serve with vegetables or a fruit pudding (pages 100–106).

Variation

Serve the chicken with or on the sweet potato, without baking it in the oven, together with the vegetables or a fruit pudding.

Dieticians' notes

- This dish contains both the protein and the starch of your meal, but only one vegetable. Simply add two cooked vegetables or a platter of roast vegetables or a large tossed salad for a balanced meal.
- Sweet potato is a good source of soluble fibre. It not only lowers cholesterol, but also lowers morning blood sugar levels in those with diabetes. The high fibre content of this meal comes from the sweet potato.
- As this meal is low in fat, a cheese sauce can be served with the vegetables, or a salad dressing can be added to the salad.

* See page 122 for the recommended product list.

Chicken and mushroom pie
Serves 6

5 chicken breasts, skinned

5 ml oil*, olive **or** canola (1 t)

1 medium onion, peeled and chopped finely

2 slices lean ham, chopped (40 g **or** ⅓ of 125 g packet) **or**
    2 strips lean bacon, all fat removed, chopped

1 clove garlic, peeled and crushed

250 g mushrooms, sliced (1 punnet)

4 courgettes (baby marrows), coarsely grated, optional

1.25 ml salt (¼ t)

2.5 ml freshly ground black pepper (½ t)

15 g mushroom soup powder (2 T or ⅓ packet)

60 ml skimmed milk* (¼ c)

300 ml boiling water (1⅕ c)

30 ml lower GI oats* (2 T)

2 sheets phyllo pastry (2 double A4 sheets)

1 egg, beaten

Nutrients per serving (without starch and vegetables)

GI low (39) • Carbohydrates 10 g • Protein 32 g
Fat 6 g • Saturated fat 1.6 g • Fibre 2 g
kJ 1 139 • GL 4
One serving is equivalent to: 4 lean protein + ½ starch + ½ vegetable

---

1. Preheat the oven to 220° C.
2. Cut the chicken breasts into small pieces.
3. Pour the oil into a large frying pan and heat on medium heat. Add the onion, ham or bacon, chicken and garlic, and gently stir-fry until brown.
4. Add the mushrooms, courgettes, salt and pepper, and cook until just tender.
5. Mix the soup powder with the milk in a cup or mug. Add some of the boiling water to fill the cup and mix well. Pour over the chicken and mushroom mixture in the frying pan. Add the rest of the water and the oats and stir until the sauce has thickened slightly.
6. Pour the pie filling into a 200 x 200 mm ovenproof dish sprayed with non-stick cooking spray.
7. Take the phyllo pastry sheets and loosely pile them in a ruffled heap on top of the chicken filling. Brush lightly with the beaten egg.
8. Turn the oven down to 180° C and bake for 15–20 minutes, until the pastry is golden and the filling is heated through.
9. Serve with a large tossed salad or two cooked vegetables to make a balanced meal. If desired, half a cup of cooked starch, such as rice, pasta, barley, etc., or a pudding (pages 100–106) can be added.

Each sheet of phyllo pastry is normally brushed with melted butter, which increases the fat and saturated fat content of a dish. However, lightly brushing the top pastry sheets with beaten egg instead, gives a lovely golden brown colour to the baked pastry.

Phyllo pastry can be stored in the deep freeze for up to three months. However, it needs to be defrosted for an hour before it is used. It can be stored in the fridge for 2–3 days.

Although any soup powder can be used, using mushroom soup powder in this recipe is quite important as this increases the mushroom flavour of the pie. Using brown mushrooms, instead of button mushrooms, will also help to increase the mushroom flavour.

Dieticians' notes

• The salad or cooked vegetables make this a balanced meal, as the pie contains only half a vegetable per serving.
• This is an ideal supper for slimmers who have been out to tea, and have had a muffin or a portion of cake. To compensate for cake, at least a starch and a fat should be omitted at the next meal. This chicken pie does just that.
• Phyllo is a useful pastry because it is fat free. However, it has a high GI, so use sparingly. This pie contains only two sheets of phyllo with other low GI ingredients, which lower the GI and GL.
• Lower GI oats have been used to thicken this dish, instead of high GI cornflour, flour or gravy powder.

* See page 122 for the recommended product list.

Mediterranean chicken stew
Serves 4

250 ml cooked lentils* (1 c) **or** 80 ml whole raw lentils*
 (⅓ c)

5 ml oil*, canola **or** olive (1 t)

4 skinless chicken thighs

4 skinless chicken drumsticks

1 large onion, peeled and chopped

1 clove garlic, peeled and chopped

1 red pepper, seeded and chopped

1 chilli, seeded and chopped, optional

750 g fresh Mediterranean vegetables (1 packet)

5 ml vegetable **or** chicken stock powder* (1 t), dissolved
 in 250 ml boiling water (1 c)

15 ml soya sauce* (1 T)

15 ml balsamic vinegar (1 T)

freshly ground black pepper

Nutrients per serving
GI low (42) • Carbohydrates 38 g • Protein 38 g
Fat 12 g • Saturated fat 3 g • Fibre 9 g
kJ 1 822 • GL 16
One serving is equivalent to: 4 lean protein
+ 1½ starch + 3 vegetables

1. If using raw lentils, cook the lentils in plenty of boiling water until done (about 40 minutes).
2. In a medium saucepan, heat the oil, add the chicken and brown it. Remove and set aside.
3. Fry the onion and garlic in the same saucepan until transparent. Add the red pepper and chilli, and stir-fry until just done.
4. Add the mixed vegetables, prepared stock, soya sauce and balsamic vinegar, and stir. Cover and cook for about 20 minutes or until the vegetables are soft.
5. Add the lentils and black pepper, and mash some of the mixed vegetables and lentils. Cook uncovered until the sauce thickens.
6. Serve as a meal.

Tinned and drained lentils (410 g tin) can be used, should you not have time to cook raw lentils.

To shorten the preparation time of this dish, precook the Mediterranean vegetables in the microwave for 10 minutes, and only cook for 3 minutes in step 4.

Mediterranean vegetables consist of brinjals (egg plant / aubergines), green and red peppers, onion, butternut and sweet potato.

Dieticians' notes
- Unless you want to carbo-load, do not add starch to this meal, as the meal already contains lentils and sweet potato.
- The original recipe contained three times the recommended amount of sodium. We had to reduce both the soya sauce and the stock powder in order to bring the sodium within the acceptable level of about 500 mg per meal. Alternatively, use sodium-reduced soya sauce.
- This recipe is exceptionally high in fibre and vegetables.

* See page 122 for the recommended product list.

Thai chicken with curried yoghurt and coriander marinade
Serves 4

4 chicken breasts, skinned and deboned
2.5 ml salt (½ t)
freshly ground black pepper
175 ml low fat plain yoghurt* (¾ c)
30 ml Thai red curry paste (2 T)
60 ml coriander leaves, chopped (¼ c)
500 ml frozen whole corn **or** 2 tins, drained (2 c)

Nutrients per serving with corn
GI low (47) • Carbohydrates 21 g • Protein 37 g
Fat 6 g • Saturated fat 1.5 g • Fibre 7 g
kJ 1 235 • GL 10
One serving is equivalent to: 4 lean protein
+ 1½ starch

1. Slice each chicken breast open lengthwise, cover with clingfilm and flatten slightly with a rolling pin or meat mallet.
2. Place the chicken in a flat casserole dish and flavour on both sides with the salt and black pepper.
3. Mix the yoghurt, curry paste and coriander to form a marinade.
4. Cover the chicken with the marinade and place in the fridge for at least 20–30 minutes.
5. Heat a griddle pan until hot, and fry all the chicken pieces on both sides until cooked through.
6. Serve hot on a bed of whole corn with two cooked vegetables, as this meal does not contain enough vegetables or fruit.

Thai curry paste and fresh coriander leaves complement each other particularly well.

Dieticians' notes
- People with high blood pressure should use frozen corn, rather than tinned, which is higher in sodium.
- The starch of this meal (corn) can be omitted and replaced by a pudding, as shown opposite.

* See page 122 for the recommended product list.

Mild Indian chicken curry with moothias (dumplings)
Serves 6

This is an aromatic mild chicken curry with an unusual starch accompaniment.

4 chicken breasts, skinned
7.5 ml ginger and garlic paste (1½ t)
5 ml turmeric powder (arad) (1 t)
5 ml coriander powder (dhania) (1 t)
5 ml chilli powder (1 t)
2.5 ml freshly ground black pepper (½ t)
15 ml oil*, sunflower **or** canola (1 T)
2 medium onions, peeled and chopped
15 ml oil*, sunflower **or** canola (1 T)
2 tomatoes, chopped
5 ml salt (1 t)
1 cinnamon stick (tuj)
4 whole cloves
500 ml fresh green beans, sliced lengthwise **or** frozen green beans (2 c)

Moothias (Dumplings)
Makes 12

500 ml spinach **or** fenugreek (bhaji), washed, drained and chopped (2 c)
1 onion, peeled and chopped
1 egg, beaten
5 ml green chillies, finely chopped (1 t), optional
2.5 ml salt (1 t)
1 ml turmeric (arad) (¼ t)
2.5 ml coriander powder (dhania) (½ t)
2.5 ml baking powder (½ t)
10 ml sugar (2 t)
90 ml maize meal (6 T)
200 ml soya flour* (⅘ c) **or** chickpea flour* (chana)
2.5 ml cumin seeds (jeero) (½ t)

Nutrients per serving with moothias (but without rice)
GI low (39) • Carbohydrates 26 g • Protein 35 g
Fat 13 g • Saturated fat 2 g • Fibre 6 g
kJ 1 509 • GL 10
One serving is equivalent to: 1 starch + 4 lean protein + 2 vegetables

1. Cut the chicken into cubes.
2. Mash all the spices together and mix with the chicken cubes. Set aside.
3. Pour the first tablespoon of oil into a large saucepan and gently fry the onions until transparent and just starting to brown.
4. Push the onions to one side of the saucepan, pour the second tablespoon of oil onto the free side and fry the chicken and spices in this, adding the onion as you stir.
5. Add the tomatoes, salt, cinnamon stick, cloves and green beans, and simmer until the chicken is almost cooked.
6. Meanwhile, prepare the moothias.
7. In a large bowl, mix all the ingredients together with a wooden spoon to make a stiff, crumbly dough, and then form into 12 dumplings with your hands.
8. Place the prepared moothias on top of the curry in the saucepan, sprinkle with 50 ml (⅕ c) of water, close the lid, and steam slowly for 30 minutes.
9. Serve the chicken with two moothias per person, as the starch, and add a large mixed salad.

If you prefer a hotter, more robust curry, double up all the spices.

Dieticians' notes
- The fibre content is high due to the soya flour and all the vegetables in the dish.
- For those who like rice, a small portion of cooked rice (½ c or 125 ml per person) can be added to this meal. The GL would then go up by 10. Instead of the rice, you could have a serving of pudding.
- This dish is relatively high in sodium, due to the addition of salt to both the curry and the moothias. Those with high blood pressure should halve the salt in the curry.

* See page 122 for the recommended product list.

Alna's creamy chicken with pasta
Serves 6

166 g pasta*, durum wheat, preferably tagliatelle
  (⅓ of 500 g packet)
2 onions, peeled and chopped
3 cloves garlic, peeled and chopped
5 ml oil*, canola **or** olive (1 t)
250 g button mushrooms, sliced (1 punnet)
220 g baked beans* (1 small tin)
380 g low fat evaporated milk* (1 tin)
440 g cooked white chicken meat **or** 4 skinned chicken
  breasts, cooked and cubed
freshly ground black pepper
10 ml Parmesan cheese (2 t)

Nutrients per serving
GI low (42) • Carbohydrates 39 g • Protein 33 g
Fat 7 g • Saturated fat 2.5 g • Fibre 0 g
kJ 1 485 • GL 16
One serving is equivalent to: 2 starch + ½ low fat dairy
+ 3 lean protein + 1 vegetable

1. Cook the pasta in lightly salted boiling water until just tender. Drain and set aside.
2. Meanwhile, fry the onions and garlic in the oil until transparent (and uncooked chicken, if using raw chicken).
3. Add the mushrooms and cook until the liquid has evaporated.
4. Place the baked beans in a liquidiser, add a little of the evaporated milk and liquidise until smooth.
5. Add the bean mixture to the onion and mushroom mixture. Use the rest of the evaporated milk to rinse the liquidiser and then add the liquid to the saucepan. Add the cooked chicken and stir continuously over low heat to reduce the liquid and thicken the mixture.
6. Serve the chicken on the pasta, sprinkled with black pepper and Parmesan.
7. Serve with vegetables, such as Roast onion, tomato and zucchini (page 84), a large salad or a fruit pudding, such as Spicy poached pears (page 100) or Caramelised fruit (page 28), as this dish does not contain enough vegetables or fruit.

If you do not have leftover cooked chicken, gently poach the chicken breasts in a little water and herbs. Alternatively, add the uncooked, cubed chicken to the saucepan, before the mushrooms, and then stir-fry with the onions and garlic until cooked.

Dieticians' notes
• This recipe is a good example of how baked beans can be used successfully as a thickener for sauces and gravies, instead of high GI, high salt soup or gravy powder.
• We used only four chicken breasts in this recipe, although it serves six people. The evaporated milk and baked beans contribute protein to the meal in addition to the concentrated source of protein provided by the chicken.
• When buying pasta, check on the list of ingredients that it is made from durum wheat, as the GI is lower than pasta made from flour. Homemade pasta also has a high GI, as it is usually made from high GI cake flour.

* See page 122 for the recommended product list.

Fish dishes

Pasta Alfredo with smoked trout or salmon
Serves 4

This is a lovely creamy pasta Alfredo, without the fat of the regular version of this dish.

166 g durum wheat tagliatelle* (⅓ of 500 g packet)
5 ml oil*, olive **or** canola (1 t)
1 large onion, peeled and chopped
200 g mushrooms, sliced (1 punnet)
2 cloves garlic, chopped
60 ml dry white wine (¼ c)
380 g low fat evaporated milk* (1 tin)
30 ml lower GI oats* (2 T)
30 ml fresh thyme, chopped (2 T)
black pepper to taste
250 g smoked trout **or** salmon*, sliced

Nutrients per serving
GI low (42) • Carbohydrates 49 g • Protein 28 g
Fat 9 g • Saturated fat 3.5 g • Fibre 5 g
kJ 1 738 • GL 20
One serving is equivalent to: 2 starch + 1 low fat dairy + 2 lean protein + 1 vegetable

---

1. Cook the pasta in plenty of lightly salted boiling water until just tender. Drain and set aside.
2. Heat the oil in a saucepan and fry the onion until transparent.
3. Add the mushrooms and stir-fry until a sauce forms. Add the garlic and stir.
4. Add the wine and cook for a few minutes to heat through.
5. Add the evaporated milk and oats, and bring to the boil. Reduce the heat and cook gently, uncovered, for 5–10 minutes until the sauce has thickened and reduced slightly.
6. Add the thyme, black pepper and fish.
7. Mix the sauce with the cooked pasta and serve immediately with a large salad and / or 2 cooked vegetables.

Fresh thyme should be added towards the end of cooking as it is a delicate herb that easily loses its flavour when cooked. Dried thyme, by contrast, can be added earlier.

Dieticians' notes
- Evaporated milk (preferably the low fat version) is a great alternative to cream, and gives a creamy taste to pasta dishes and soups, minus the fat.
- We used lower GI oats as thickener instead of the more commonly used high GI flour, cornflour or gravy powder.
- Although the fat is slightly higher than we usually aim for when fish is used, salmon and trout are both fatty fishes that contain valuable omega-3 fatty acids, especially long-chain DHA and EPA, of which most of us consume far too little. Try to consume fatty fish at least twice a week, in order to get in enough omega-3s, which improve concentration and protect against inflammatory and lifestyle diseases.

* See page 122 for the recommended product list.

Honey and mustard baked salmon with roast sweet potatoes and onion

Serves 4

2–3 small sweet potatoes, peeled and sliced thickly
  (400g)
2 small onions, peeled and cubed
1–2 cloves garlic, chopped finely
10 ml oil*, olive **or** canola (2 t)
20 ml honey (4 t)
7.5 ml mustard powder (1½ t)
1 sprig fresh rosemary, leaves chopped
500 g fresh salmon steaks **or** fillets*

Nutrients per serving
GI low (55) • Carbohydrates 32 g • Protein 22 g
Fat 13 g • Saturated fat 4 g • Fibre 4 g
kJ 1 472 • GL 18
One serving is equivalent to: 2 starch + 2½ protein

1. Preheat the oven to 180° C.
2. In the microwave, cook the sweet potatoes, onions and garlic in boiling water for 10–15 minutes and drain. Alternatively, cook in a saucepan on the stove.
3. Place the oil in an ovenproof dish that is large enough for the sweet potato and onions, and heat for a few minutes in the oven.
4. Place the cooked sweet potatoes and onions in the ovenproof dish and toss lightly to cover with the oil. Bake for 10–15 minutes.
5. Meanwhile, mix the honey, mustard powder and rosemary in a cup and microwave for 15 seconds on high to melt the honey, or place the cup into a bowl of boiling water until the honey has melted.
6. Spread most of the honey, mustard and rosemary mixture over the fish fillets, but reserve a little for serving.
7. Spray a cooling rack with non-stick cooking spray and suspend it over the sweet potato and onion dish.
8. Place the fish directly onto the cooling rack, suspended over the dish of sweet potatoes and onions, so that the drippings of the fish can fall onto the sweet potatoes.
9. Bake the fish and sweet potato for 10–15 minutes.
10. Spread the rest of the honey and mustard mixture on the fish and serve with lots of cooked vegetables.

Cooked deep orange sweet potato, which can be mistaken for butternut, goes well with salmon. (Note the orange sweet potato in the photo.) Marina's aubergine towers (page 88) go particularly well with this dish.

Dieticians' notes
- Salmon is an excellent source of omega-3 poly-unsaturated fatty acids that help prevent blood clotting and inflammatory disease, and improve concentration. For this reason the slightly higher fat content is well worth it. No more fat should be added to the starch and vegetables of this meal. Alternatively, reduce your fat intake during the rest of the day.
- It is recommended that fatty fish, such as salmon, trout, pilchards, mackerel, etc., is eaten twice a week.
- Sweet potato is a healthier option than chips or mashed potato.

* See page 122 for the recommended product list.

Hake and basil pesto stir-fry
Serves 4

Prepare and cook the rice and vegetables or salad to be served with this meal before you start cooking this dish, so that all can be served as one meal.

185 ml low GI rice* (¾ c)
2.5 ml salt (½ t)
5 ml oil*, olive **or** canola (1 t)
1 green, yellow **or** red pepper, halved and sliced
1 large onion, halved and sliced
400–500 g hake medallions, cut into cubes
black pepper to taste
125 ml basil pesto (½ c) – see recipe below

Nutrients per serving with rice
GI low (44) • Carbohydrates 29 g • Protein 26 g
Fat 11 g • Saturated fat 2 g • Fibre 2 g
kJ 1 373 • GL 13
One serving is equivalent to: 1½ starch
+ 3 lean protein + ½ fat + 1 vegetable

1. Cook the rice with the salt in plenty of boiling water until done.
2. Heat the oil in a non-stick frying pan and stir-fry the peppers and onion slices on high until slightly browned. Remove from the pan and keep to one side.
3. Add the hake cubes to the pan and stir-fry on high for about 5 minutes, until all the pieces are cooked through. Add the black pepper while stir-frying. Be careful not to overcook the fish.
4. Add the basil pesto, onion and sweet peppers and gently toss until well mixed.
5. Reduce heat and cover the pan. Simmer for about 3 minutes, until a sauce forms. Add a little water if necessary.
6. Serve with the rice and two cooked vegetables or a large tossed salad.

Add basil towards the end of cooking, as heat destroys the aroma of fresh basil. Chopped fresh basil leaves can be successfully frozen in ice cubes for inclusion in cooked dishes at the last minute.

Dieticians' note
Although this hake and basil pesto stir-fry contains quite a bit of mostly beneficial fat, each serving of the dish still supplies only 11 g of fat, which is an acceptable fat level for a meal. This is due to the low fat fish. For this reason, no more fat should be added to the starch and vegetables of this meal.

Basil pesto
Makes 125 ml (½ c) or 4 servings (30 ml or 2 T)

This pesto can also be used with pasta dishes and salads.

500 ml fresh basil, broken into pieces (2 c) (60 g)
3 to 4 cloves garlic, roughly chopped
15 ml pine nuts (1 T)
5 ml Parmesan cheese, finely grated (1 t)
30 ml olive oil* (2 T)
30 ml water (2 T)

Nutrients per serving – 30 ml or 2 T
GI low (< 30) • Carbohydrates 1.2 g • Protein 1 g
Fat 8 g • Saturated fat 1.3 g • Fibre 1 g
kJ 348 • GL n/a
One serving is equivalent to: 2 fat

1. Combine all the ingredients in a food processor and process for 1 to 2 minutes. Season lightly with salt and pepper.
2. Store the pesto in an airtight container in the fridge until needed. Preferably use within 2–3 days.

Add the stems of the basil for extra flavour.
Make the pesto beforehand and refrigerate for at least 12 hours for the flavours to develop.

Dieticians' notes
• Most pestos are extremely high in fat, 60% fat or higher, as the main ingredients are oil, pine nuts and Parmesan cheese – all essential ingredients that give pesto its traditional flavour. This adapted pesto recipe is still packed with flavour, but without all the unnecessary fat – 24% fat.
• If possible, try to use cold pressed, extra virgin olive oil. Apart from the fact that it adds flavour to the pesto, it is also full of natural vitamin E and other antioxidants that protect against modern lifestyle diseases.

* See page 122 for the recommended product list.

Moroccan hake fillets

Serves 4

600 g frozen **or** fresh hake fillets (4 x 150 g)

30 ml olive oil* (2 T)

10 ml crushed garlic (2 t) (3 cloves)

7.5 ml ground cumin (1½ t)

5 ml paprika (1 t)

pinch of cayenne pepper

1 bunch coriander leaves (dhania), finely chopped

30 ml lemon juice (2 T)

60 ml water (to thin out the sauce, if needed)

Nutrients per serving including baby potatoes
GI intermediate (58) • Carbohydrates 23 g
Protein 29 g • Fat 9 g • Saturated fat 1.2 g
Fibre 2 g • kJ 1 203 • GL 13
One serving is equivalent to: 1 starch + 4 lean protein

1. Preheat the oven to 200° C.
2. Place the hake fillets on a lightly greased baking sheet.
3. Mix the oil, garlic, cumin, paprika, cayenne pepper, coriander leaves and lemon juice in a bowl. Add some of the water if the mixture is too thick to spread easily over the fish.
4. Spread the spice mixture evenly over the fish fillets.
5. Place in the oven. Turn the heat down to 180° C and bake for 15–20 minutes, until the hake flesh flakes when you insert a fork.
6. Serve with baby potatoes (three per person), a salad such as John's warm tomato salad (page 46) and two cooked vegetables.

This fish topping is salty enough so that no additional salt or pepper is needed. This makes Moroccan herbs ideal for using in salt- or sodium-controlled dishes. Ground cumin and fresh coriander leaves give the typical Moroccan flavour.

Any lean fish such as Cape Whiting or kingklip can be used instead of the hake.

Dieticians' notes

- With a GL of only 13, it is quite acceptable to have a fruit-based pudding with this meal (see the recipes in the pudding section).
- With hake being a very lean fish, it is acceptable to use more beneficial fat in its preparation. In this case, we have used more olive oil than we would normally to enhance the flavour of the topping, while still keeping the total fat within the recommended limit.
- The sodium of this dish is particularly low and thus is ideal for those suffering from high blood pressure.

* See page 122 for the recommended product list.

The low down on fish

White fish, such as:
- hake
- kingklip
- Cape Whiting
- sole

are some of the leanest sources of protein. Fresh tuna and canned tuna in brine are also extremely low in fat. Unfortunately, when these fish are served in restaurants, they are usually covered in a fatty batter or crumbed or grilled with lots of butter and / or oil, resulting in a high fat meal. In addition, fish is usually served with chips, adding even more fat to the meal. Always ask for fish to be grilled without added oil or butter and the sauce on the side. Choose rice, baby potatoes, sweet potato or pasta as your starch. Remember to have a large mixed salad as your starter and ask for the dressing to be served separately. The best sources of omega-3 essential fatty acids (EPA and DHA) are:
- salmon – fresh, smoked or canned
- mackerel – smoked or canned

- trout – fresh or smoked
- herring
- kippers
- pilchards
- sardines
- anchovies

Omega-3 fatty acids make up the bulk of every cell membrane, particularly that of the brain and the retina of the eye, and thus they are important for brain function. In children, they help in the management of AD(H)D, and in adults they help to delay or prevent the onset of Alzheimer's. They are also anti-inflammatory and therefore play a role in the management of allergies, asthma, hay fever, gout, arthritis and multiple sclerosis. Omega-3s are also cardio-protective as they prevent excessive blood clotting and help to reduce blood pressure. In addition, they help to protect against insulin resistance, excessive weight and diabetes.

For the above reasons, we should all make a particular effort to eat omega-3-rich fish and other fish twice a week.

Vegetarian and vegetable dishes

Risotto
Serves 4

1 medium onion, peeled and chopped

5 ml oil*, olive **or** canola (1 t)

2 celery stalks, chopped

3 medium carrots, peeled and sliced into discs

500 ml boiling water (2 c)

10 ml vegetable stock powder* (2 t)

250 ml Arborio (risotto) rice (1 c)

175 ml dry white wine (¾ c)

250 ml frozen peas (1 c)

90 g lower fat cheese*, grated (size of three matchboxes
   before grating)

15 ml Parmesan cheese (3 t)

60 ml low fat milk* (¼ c)

15 ml lemon juice (1 T)

freshly ground black pepper

Nutrients per serving

GI intermediate (61) • Carbohydrates 41 g
Protein 14 g • Fat 7 g • Saturated fat 3.7 g
Fibre 7 g • kJ 1 251 • GL 25
One serving is equivalent to: 2 starch + 1½ protein
+ 2 vegetables

---

1. Fry the onion in the oil in a large frying pan on medium heat. Add the celery and carrots, and fry for a further 3–5 minutes.
2. Pour the boiling water into another saucepan, add the stock powder and stir until dissolved. Keep warm on low heat.
3. Add the uncooked rice to the pan with the vegetables. Fry for 3 minutes.
4. Add the white wine and allow the rice to absorb it. Then add the warm prepared stock, ensuring that the rice is covered by liquid. Simmer covered for about 25 minutes, stirring occasionaly. Add boiling water if it becomes too dry. Bear in mind that the end product should be creamy.
5. Once the risotto is creamy, stir in the peas, grated cheeses, milk and lemon juice. Allow the cheese to melt. Add black pepper to taste.
6. Serve immediately, preferably with a salad.

Non-vegetarian variation

Halve the lower fat cheese and add one packet (250 g) lower fat, lower salt bacon. Remove the fat, chop and fry in a non-stick frying pan sprayed with non-stick cooking spray. Add 15 ml (1 T) raw honey and fry until crisp and brown. In addition, the stock powder should be reduced to 5 ml (1 t), to control the sodium (salt) content.

Dieticians' notes

- Although Arborio rice has a higher GI than most rice, the vegetables in this recipe help to bring down the GI to an acceptable intermediate GI value. However, those with diabetes should preferably have this supper dish only after having done at least one hour's exercise in the afternoon.
- This recipe already contains enough sodium, so don't be tempted to add salt at table, particularly if you have high blood pressure.
- The high fibre content is provided by the vegetables, as Arborio rice is quite low in fibre.
- Although this dish is not very high in fat, unlike traditional vegetarian recipes, slightly more than half of the fat is saturated, as most of the fat comes from the cheeses.
- Using the bacon variation gives roughly the same nutritional analysis, except that the sodium content is higher.

* See page 122 for the recommended product list.

Lentil moussaka

Serves 4

A delicious dish for vegetarians who enjoy milk and eggs.

150 ml split **or** red lentils* (⅗ c)

2 large tomatoes, chopped

60 ml tomato purée (4 T)

1 clove garlic, peeled and crushed

2.5 ml dried oregano (½ t) **or** 7.5 ml fresh oregano (½ T)

pinch of nutmeg

10 ml vegetable stock powder* (2 t)

250 ml boiling water (1 c)

5 ml sugar (1 t), if the tomatoes are too tart

30 ml oil*, olive **or** canola (2 T)

2 medium aubergines (brinjals), topped and tailed

1 onion, peeled and chopped

2.5 ml salt (½ t)

1 egg

200 g fat free cottage cheese* (1 tub)

freshly ground black pepper

pinch of nutmeg

> **Nutrients per serving**
> GI low (34) • Carbohydrates 26 g • Protein 19 g
> Fat 9 g • Saturated fat 2 g • Fibre 10 g
> kJ 1 211 • GL 9
> One serving is equivalent to: 1 starch + 2 lean protein
> + 1 fat + 2 vegetables

1. Place the lentils in a saucepan with the tomatoes, tomato purée, garlic, oregano and nutmeg.
2. Add the vegetable stock powder.
3. Pour the boiling water over and simmer covered for 20 minutes. Add the sugar if too tart.
4. Preheat the oven to 180° C. Wash and thickly slice the unpeeled aubergines.
5. In a frying pan, heat one tablespoon of the oil over medium heat and lightly fry the aubergine slices, adding about 50 ml (⅕ c) of water to the pan to prevent burning. Remove from the pan and set aside.
6. Heat the other tablespoon of oil in the same frying pan and gently fry the onion until just starting to brown, stirring all the time. Add the salt and stir through.
7. In a lightly greased oven-proof dish, layer half the aubergine slices at the bottom. Top evenly with two thirds of the fried onion. Spoon all the lentil mixture onto the onion. Sprinkle the rest of the onion onto the lentils, and place the leftover aubergine slices on top.
8. Beat the egg and cottage cheese together, and season with the pepper and nutmeg.
9. Pour evenly over the moussaka, and bake for 30–40 minutes. Then place under a hot grill for a few minutes until the topping is golden brown.
10. Serve with a salad to make a balanced meal.

When cooking vegetables, keep the water to use instead of the stock powder and boiling water. Use 250 ml of the vegetable water with half a teaspoon of salt for this recipe.

Dieticians' notes

- It is important to use fat free cottage cheese in this dish, and to use only 15 ml (1 T) of oil to fry the brinjals. This keeps the fat content well within the recommended limit. Most vegetarian dishes are higher in fat, as more oil and / or high fat cheese is required to give a good flavour profile to a dish made predominantly with legumes that are dry and bland.
- The exceptionally high fibre content is provided by the lentils and brinjals.
- As this main meal dish contains only one starch and two protein, it would be quite acceptable to have one serving of Apricot cheesecake (page 108) for dessert.

* See page 122 for the recommended product list.

Roast tomato, onion and zucchini
Serves 4

15 ml olive oil* (3 t)

4 medium onions, halved and sliced

15 ml fresh thyme, chopped (1 T)

2.5 ml salt (½ t)

8 plum tomatoes, cut lengthwise into four **or** 4 regular
tomatoes, quartered

10–12 zucchini (baby marrow), sliced diagonally into 1 cm
pieces (300 g)

black pepper to taste

Nutrients per serving
GI low (< 30) • Carbohydrates 19 g • Protein 3 g
Fat 4 g • Saturated fat 0.6 g • Fibre 5 g
kJ 579 • GL 5
One serving is equivalent to: 3 vegetables + 1 fat

1. Preheat the oven to 180° C.
2. In a non-stick frying pan, heat one teaspoon of the oil over medium heat. Add the onions and fry, stirring continuously for 10 minutes or until tender.
3. Add the thyme and half of the salt. Stir and set aside.
4. Arrange the tomato, onion and zucchini slices in rows across the length or width of a shallow, rectangular baking dish.
5. Sprinkle with the rest of the salt, black pepper and oil (10 ml). Cover tightly with foil (shiny side down) and bake for 30 minutes.
6. Bake uncovered for a further 15 minutes or until the vegetables are tender. Allow to stand for 10 minutes before serving.
7. Serve as the vegetables with any meal.

Oregano or basil is most often used with tomato, but thyme is also a good companion. The amount of fresh thyme used might seem a lot, but it is a mild herb and can thus be used liberally.

Dieticians' note

This is an ideal dish to serve with a meal that traditionally contains only starch and protein, like macaroni cheese. However, remember to use less fat in the protein and starch dish, as this vegetable dish contains a fat portion.

Curried sweet potato
Serves 10

It is worth making this large recipe, as it freezes very well. Make and freeze in single servings, ready to defrost and use at a moments notice.

4 medium sweet potatoes (about 1 kg)

2 medium onions, peeled and chopped

10 ml olive oil* (2 t)

10–15 ml masala **or** curry powder (2–3 t)

1 large green apple, peeled and grated

10 ml good quality apricot jam (2 t)

15 ml fresh lemon juice (1 T)

1.25 ml salt (¼ t)

250 ml water (1 c)

10 ml soft brown sugar (2 t)

Nutrients per serving
GI low (50) • Carbohydrates 28 g • Protein 2 g
Fat 1 g • Saturated fat 0.2 g • Fibre 4 g
kJ 606 • GL 14
One serving is equivalent to: 1½ starch + 1 vegetable

1. Scrub the sweet potatoes and then boil in their skins until tender. Alternatively, prick a few times with a fork and cook in the microwave until tender.
2. Meanwhile, gently fry the onions in the oil until transparent.
3. Add the masala or curry powder and fry for another few minutes to develop the flavour.
4. Add the apple, jam, lemon juice, salt, water and sugar. Cook for a few minutes and set aside.
5. Preheat the oven to 180° C and spray a medium casserole dish with non-stick cooking spray.
6. Peel the cooked and cooled sweet potatoes and cut into cubes.
7. Place in the lightly greased casserole dish and spoon the curry mix over the sweet potatoes. Alternatively mash the two together.
8. Bake, uncovered for 30–45 minutes.
9. Serve as a starch with any main meal.

Dieticians' notes

- Most people do not get close to the 30–40 g of fibre recommended per day. Sweet potatoes are a good source of fibre (especially soluble fibre, which binds cholesterol and delays gastric emptying, thereby lowering the GI). Including one serving of this dish with any main meal will, together with the vegetables, supply an ample amount of fibre for that meal.
- Remember that one serving of this dish is equivalent to one and a half starch, so preferably add it only to those meals that contain half a starch.
- Add only vegetables and protein to one serving of this dish, in order to make a balanced meal.

* See page 122 for the recommended product list.

Chickpea and apple curry
Serves 4

3 Granny Smith apples
15 ml oil*, olive **or** canola (1 T)
2 medium onions, peeled and chopped
5 ml mustard seeds (1 t)
10 ml masala (2 t)
5 ml turmeric (1 t)
5 ml cumin (1 t)
300 ml chickpeas*, cooked (1⅕ c) **or** 410 g tin, drained
10 ml vegetable stock powder* (2 t)
2.5 ml salt (½ t)
freshly ground black pepper
125 ml lite coconut milk* (½ c)
400 ml water (1⅗ c)
fresh coriander leaves (dhania)

Nutrients per serving
GI low (31) • Carbohydrates 33 g • Protein 6 g
Fat 7 g • Saturated fat 2 g • Fibre 7 g
kJ 933 • GL 10
One serving is equivalent to: 1 starch + 1 lean protein
+ ½ fat + 1 fruit + 1 vegetable

1. Peel and grate two of the apples.
2. Heat the oil in a large frying pan and add the grated apples and chopped onions and fry until soft, but not golden.
3. Add the spices to the onion and apple and fry for 1 minute.
4. Add the cooked chickpeas, chicken stock powder, salt and pepper.
5. Add the coconut milk and water, and simmer covered until the curry has a creamy texture (about 45 minutes).
6. Peel and slice the third apple. Add to the curry.
7. Heat through, mixing well.
8. Garnish with fresh coriander leaves and serve immediately with a large tossed salad to which 30 ml (2 T) nuts or 100 g tofu (size of three matchboxes) have been added, to make a complete meal.

Coriander adds an interesting note to the flavour of curries.

Dieticians' notes

- Tinned chickpeas, although convenient, should not be used by those with high blood pressure as the sodium content of this dish would then be too high. Rather soak a large quantity of dry chickpeas overnight, and then cook for two hours and freeze in 300 ml (230 g) batches for use in vegetarian dishes and as salad sprinkles.
- We recommend adding only two tablespoons of nuts to the salad that goes with this meal, because this adds almost a whole fat portion but only one third of a protein portion per serving. This goes to show that nuts, although they are sources of good fats, should be eaten only in small amounts and should not regularly be used as a source of protein. The tofu also adds only a third of a protein portion, but much less fat than the nuts. This shows that you have to eat lots of tofu to get a little bit of protein.
- Adding a small tub of soy yoghurt as pudding would be the most efficient way to increase the protein content of this meal, as this will add one whole portion of protein (and not just a third).
- Coconut milk adds a lot of flavour to curried dishes. However, most of the fat in coconut milk is saturated fat, and for this reason we used the lite version – only half a cup in the whole recipe. Freeze the rest of the tin for later use.

* See page 122 for the recommended product list.

Lentils in paprika and wine sauce
Serves 4

150 ml brown lentils*, uncooked (⅗ c)

10 ml oil*, olive **or** canola (2 t)

2 large onions, peeled and chopped

2 cloves garlic, peeled and crushed

2 carrots, peeled and cut into thin discs

4 celery stalks with leaves, chopped

8 baby potatoes, washed and sliced

2 bay leaves

200 ml white wine (⅘ c)

15 ml vegetable stock powder* (1 T)

250 ml boiling water (1 c)

10 ml ground paprika (2 t)

10 ml cumin, whole **or** ground (2 t)

2.5 ml salt (½ t)

2 tomatoes, cut into eighths

Nutrients per serving
GI low (40) • Carbohydrates 43 g • Protein 13 g
Fat 3 g • Saturated fat 0.4 g • Fibre 12 g
kJ 1 197 • GL 17
One serving is equivalent to: 2 starch
+ 1½ lean protein + 2 vegetables

1. Place the lentils in a large bowl and pour boiling water over them. Leave to soften in the water for at least 30 minutes.
2. Meanwhile, heat the olive oil in a large saucepan. Add the onion, garlic, vegetables and baby potatoes, and stir-fry for about 5 minutes.
3. Add the bay leaves, white wine and the drained softened lentils to the vegetables, and cook covered on low for 10 minutes.
4. Add the stock, paprika, cumin, salt and tomatoes and cook covered for another 10 minutes.
5. Serve as a meal. Alternatively, leave out the baby potatoes and serve with one serving of the Curried sweet potato (page 84).

Dieticians' note

The exceptionally high fibre content is due to the lentils. All legumes are good sources of fibre and thus lower cholesterol effectively, protect against blood clotting (thrombosis) and help to keep you regular

Aubergine towers
Serves 4

½ packet sun-dried tomatoes (30 g)

15 ml oil*, olive **or** canola (1 T)

2–3 medium aubergines / brinjals, sliced (about 20 slices)

rocket **or** lettuce leaves, optional

1 fat reduced Feta round*, crumbled (90 g)

60 ml sweet chilli sauce (¼ c or 4 T)

2 kebab (sosatie) sticks, broken in half, **or** 4 toothpicks

Nutrients per serving
GI low (39) • Carbohydrates 18 g • Protein 6 g
Fat 9 g • Saturated fat 4 g • Fibre 5 g
kJ 755 • GL 7
One serving is equivalent to: ½ starch + ½ protein
+ 1 fat + 2 vegetables

1. Soak the sun-dried tomatoes in boiling water until soft and set aside.
2. Spray a large non-stick frying pan with non-stick cooking spray. Heat half of the oil in the pan and fry half of the aubergine slices on fairly high heat on both sides until brown. Keep turning so that they do not burn. Set aside. Add the other half of the oil to the pan and fry the rest of the aubergine slices, using the same method. Set aside.
3. Make a bed of rocket or lettuce on each of the four plates.
4. Place an aubergine slice on the rocket or lettuce, spread with some chilli sauce, sprinkle with a bit of Feta and place a few sun-dried tomatoes on top. Repeat the layers to form a tower. Try to distribute all the ingredients evenly between the towers of five slices of aubergine each.
5. Push half a sosatie stick or a toothpick through each tower to stabilise it.
6. Serve as a starter or vegetable with any meal.

Dieticians' notes
• This dish makes an ideal hors d'oeuvre because it contains mainly vegetables. However, the fat content of the meal will have to be kept low, as this "vegetable" contains one fat per serving.
• If you use 60 ml (¼ c) of basil pesto (page 76) instead of the chilli sauce, the fat content of this dish doubles. Therefore serve it with a meal that is very low in fat – less than 5 g of fat per meal. The commercial basil pesto is about 60% fat. In addition, plenty of oil is usually used to fry aubergines and the amount of Feta cheese is not necessarily controlled.

* See page 122 for the recommended product list.

Meat dishes

Pork fillet with mushrooms
Serves 4

10 ml oil*, olive **or** canola (2 t)
500 g pork fillet, sliced thickly into medallions
1 medium onion, peeled and chopped
250 g fresh mushrooms, sliced (1 punnet)
1 clove garlic, crushed
125 ml water (½ c), mixed with
  30 ml wine (2 T), optional
30 ml low fat evaporated milk * (2 T)
2.5 ml salt (½ t)
freshly ground black pepper

Nutrients per serving with baby potatoes
GI low (52) • Carbohydrates 23 g • Protein 31 g
Fat 10 g • Saturated fat 4 g • Fibre 3 g
kJ 1 446 • GL 12
One serving is equivalent to: 1 starch + 4 lean protein
+ 1 vegetable

1. Heat the oil over medium heat in a large frying pan and brown the pork on both sides. Move the cooked meat onto one side of the pan.
2. Add the onion and mushrooms and gently fry until almost cooked. Add the garlic and stir-fry for half a minute.
3. Pour the water (and wine) onto the onions and mushrooms in the pan and mix. Cook until half the liquid has evaporated.
4. Switch the stove plate off and pour the evaporated milk onto the onions and mushrooms, and stir to make a thickened sauce.
5. Move the meat back into the sauce and season with the salt and pepper.
6. Serve with two cooked vegetables and three baby potatoes per person. Alternatively, cook durum wheat pasta (166 g or ⅓ of 500 g packet of raw pasta for four servings) or Basmati rice (¾ c of raw rice for four servings) in lightly salted water.

Dieticians' notes
- Most red meat is high in fat. We have chosen to use one of the leanest red meat cuts – pork fillet in a controlled portion size – so that the fat content remains within the recommendations of 13 g per serving.
- Low fat evaporated milk adds flavour and creaminess to sauces, and can be used instead of cream in most recipes.

Barbecue sauce
Makes 6 servings (45 ml – 3 level T)

15 ml oil*, canola **or** olive (1 T)
2 medium onions, halved and sliced
1 clove garlic, crushed
30 ml soya sauce (2 T)
2 tomatoes, peeled and chopped
15 ml Muscovado **or** soft brown sugar (1 T)
30 ml Worcestershire sauce (2 T)
15 ml tomato sauce (1 T)
5 ml prepared mustard (1 t) **or** 15 ml honey and
  mustard dressing (1 T)
black pepper
125 ml water (½ c)
5 ml cornflour (1 t)

Nutrients per serving (excluding the meat)
GI low (35) • Carbohydrates 10 g • Protein 2 g
Fat 3 g • Saturated fat 0.3 g • Fibre 1 g
kJ 325 • GL 3
One serving barbecue sauce is equivalent to:
½ starch + ½ fat + 1 vegetable

1. Heat the oil in a medium saucepan and stir-fry the onions on medium high heat for about 10 minutes to caramelise the onions, without crisping them. Be sure to stir continuously.
2. Add the rest of the ingredients, except the cornflour, and simmer uncovered on low for 20 minutes, until half the liquid has evaporated.
3. Mix the cornflour with a little water in a cup and add to the sauce. Stir and boil to thicken.
4. Serve 45 ml (3 level T) per person with grilled steak (the size of the palm of your hand) or low fat meatballs, together with vegetables or salad.

Variation
For a monkeygland sauce, replace the soya sauce with 15 ml (1 T) of vinegar and add another 15 ml (1 T) of tomato sauce. Also replace the honey and mustard dressing with the same amount of chutney.

Dieticians' notes
- Soya sauce is very high in sodium and therefore no salt should be added to a meal that contains this sauce. People with high blood pressure should use half the amount of soya sauce, that is, 15 ml (1 T), or better still, opt for the monkeygland version, which contains half the amount of sodium.
- The half portion of starch is due to the presence of all the sauces, as most commercial sauces contain modified starch and sugar, making them starch-based and higher GI. Some sauces are also high in fat.

* See page 122 for the recommended product list.

MEAT DISHES

Lamb breyani
Serves 6

Plan for this dish in advance, as the rice and lentils have to be cooked first, and the meat has to marinate for two hours. Once you have done this, the rest is easy!

150 ml fat free plain yoghurt* (⅗ c)

30 ml garlic and ginger paste (2 T)

60 ml fresh coriander leaves (dhania), chopped (4 T) **or** 30 ml (2 T) dried coriander leaves

500 g extra lean lamb, fat removed and cubed

125 ml brown lentils*, uncooked (½ c) **or** 300 ml cooked **or** tinned lentils* (1 tin, drained)

1.25 ml salt (¼ t)

125 ml Basmati rice* (½ c)

1.25 ml salt (¼ t)

2.5 ml turmeric (arad) (½ t)

2.5 ml cumin seeds (jeero) (½ t) **or** 5 ml ground cumin (1 t)

2 whole cloves **or** 1.25 ml ground cloves (¼ t)

2 cardamom pods (elachi) **or** 2.5 ml ground cardamom (½ t)

15 ml oil*, sunflower **or** canola (1 T)

2 large onions, peeled and sliced, or chopped if you prefer

2 sticks cinnamon **or** 5 ml ground cinnamon (1 t)

4 whole cloves **or** 2.5 ml ground cloves (½ t)

2.5 ml cumin seeds (jeero) (½ t) **or** 5 ml ground cumin (1 t)

2 cardamom pods (elachi) **or** 2.5 ml ground cardamom (½ t)

2 tomatoes, finely chopped

1.25 ml salt (¼ t)

Nutrients per serving
GI low (34) • Carbohydrates 31 g • Protein 30 g
Fat 8 g • Saturated fat 2 g • Fibre 7 g
kJ 1 318 • GL 10
One serving is equivalent to: 1½ starch + 3 protein + 1 vegetable

---

1. In a bowl, mix the yoghurt, garlic and ginger paste, and coriander leaves.
2. Add the lamb and mix well. Refrigerate for two hours.
3. Meanwhile, cook the lentils in 375 ml (1½ c) of water and the first 1.25 ml (¼ t) of salt until soft but still firm (about 45 minutes).
4. In another saucepan, cook the rice in 375 ml (1½ c) of water with the second 1.25 ml (¼ t) of salt, turmeric, cumin, cloves and cardamom pods until done (about 30 minutes).
5. When cooked, mix the rice and lentils together and set aside.
6. Heat the oil in a heavy pan and fry the onion with the cinnamon sticks, cloves, cumin and cardamom until golden brown. Stir continuously, particularly if using ground spices.
7. Add the marinated lamb and mix well. Add the chopped tomato and salt, and cook covered for another 30 minutes. Preheat the oven to 180° C while the breyani meat mixture is cooking.
8. Place alternate layers of the rice and lentil mixture and the lamb in a deep casserole dish, starting and ending with rice and lentils. Cover and bake for 20 minutes.
9. Serve with assorted sambals and salads or sliced banana in lemon juice, chopped tomato and onion and chutney, if desired.

Garlic and ginger paste is readily available at most supermarkets in the fresh vegetable section.

Cook a double amount of rice and lentils and freeze half for the next time you want to prepare this dish.

Traditionally, this dish is made with whole spices, but using the ground spices makes a dish that is just as delicious.

Variation
Serve the lamb breyani on the rice and lentil mixture without baking it. If you choose to do this, the cooking time is shortened, but you need to cook the meat uncovered for the last 15 minutes, unless you want a thin gravy.

Dieticians' notes
• Although red meat – particularly lamb, which contains a lot of marbled fat – is usually higher in fat, the fat content can be kept within recommended limits if the portion sizes are controlled, extra lean cuts are used and all fat is removed before cooking. We used only 500 g of lean mutton or lamb for six portions. We have "diluted" the meat with the lentils, and in so doing have also greatly increased the fibre content of the dish.
• Lentils not only contribute large amounts of fibre, they also effectively lower the GI of any meal and contribute to its protein content.

* See page 122 for the recommended product list.

Quick vegetable savoury mince
Serves 4

5 ml oil*, olive **or** canola (1 t)
1 large onion, peeled and chopped
450 g extra lean mince, topside **or** ostrich
250 g mushrooms, sliced (1 punnet)
500 ml mixed vegetables, fresh **or** frozen (2 c)
10 ml beef stock powder* (2 t)
1 clove garlic, peeled and crushed
1 sprig fresh rosemary, chopped
1.25 ml ground cloves (¼ t)
15 ml vinegar (1 T)
15 ml chutney (1 T)
15 ml Worcestershire sauce (1 T)
15 ml tomato sauce (1 T)
freshly ground black pepper, to taste
4 slices low GI bread*

Nutrients per serving
GI low (46) • Carbohydrates 34 g • Protein 30 g
Fat 13 g • Saturated fat 4.5 g • Fibre 10 g
kJ 1 600 • GL 16
One serving is equivalent to: 2 starch + 3 protein
+ 1 vegetable

1. Heat the oil in a large frying pan and sauté the chopped onions until transparent.
2. Add the mince and stir-fry until browned.
3. Add the mushrooms, mixed vegetables, stock powder, garlic, rosemary, cloves, vinegar, chutney, Worcestershire sauce and tomato sauce and simmer, covered for about 20 minutes.
4. Season to taste with the black pepper.
5. Serve on one slice of low GI toast per person, together with some more vegetables or salad.

Rosemary is a very strong herb and should therefore be used in small amounts. It can also be added close to the beginning of cooking, as it does not lose its flavour during cooking, as with other fresh herbs. Rosemary also goes very well with garlic.

Dieticians' notes
• There is no need to butter the bread as the dish already contains enough fat.
• This is a quick and easy, yet balanced meal, which contains at least one portion of vegetables per person, unlike so many other mince dishes, which are practically devoid of vegetables and fibre.
• We could use only 450 g of extra lean / topside mince, otherwise the fat content of the dish would have been too high. Replacing some or all of the mince with ostrich mince will lower the fat and sodium content. If ostrich mince alone is used, you could even use 500 g of mince, instead of the 450 g we used in this recipe.
• Even though this recipe contains vegetables, they are not sufficient to lower the GI of regular, high GI brown bread. In South Africa we are now spoilt for choice with many brands of low GI breads, making it easy to use low GI bread in this recipe. When brown bread is used, the GI goes up to 60 and the GL to 21.
• This dish contains slightly more than the sodium recommendations of not more than 500 mg per meal. People with hypertension should omit the Worcestershire sauce.

* See page 122 for the recommended product list.

Mince and rice casserole
Serves 6

5 ml oil*, olive **or** canola (1 t)

1 large onion, peeled and chopped

400 g extra lean, topside **or** ostrich mince*

1 tin mushrooms, stems and pieces, drained (285 g) **or**
   1 punnet fresh mushrooms (250 g)

500 ml cooked lower GI rice* (2 c) – use ¾ c uncooked
   rice to make 2 c cooked rice

30 ml chutney (2 T)

1 tin concentrated soup, minestrone (410 g) **or** ⅓ packet
   minestrone soup powder (15 g) mixed with 125 ml
   boiling water (½ c)

750 ml mixed vegetables, fresh **or** frozen (3 c)

30 g cheese*, lower fat, grated (size of one matchbox)

Nutrients per serving
GI low (51) • Carbohydrates 29 g • Protein 25 g
Fat 11 g • Saturated fat 4 g • Fibre 6 g
kJ 1 311 • GL 15
One serving is equivalent to: 1 starch + 3 protein
+ 1½ vegetables

1. Preheat the oven to 200° C.
2. Heat the oil in a frying pan and fry the onion until transparent. Add the mince and fry until slightly browned. Add the mushrooms and stir-fry until cooked.
3. Lightly grease a large ovenproof dish with non-stick cooking spray and spoon the mince mixture evenly into the bottom.
4. Layer the cooked rice over the mince mixture.
5. Mix the chutney with the soup and pour evenly over the layers.
6. Place the dish in the oven and bake covered for 20 minutes.
7. Meanwhile, prepare the mixed vegetables by cooking them in boiling water until tender.
8. After the dish has baked for 20 minutes, spread the vegetables evenly on top of the rice and top with the cheese. Bake uncovered for another 5 minutes or until the cheese is melted.
9. Serve with a large tossed salad or a cooked vegetable.

Any flavour of soup or soup powder can be used – it does not have to be minestrone.

Dieticians' note
Make sure that you use only the matchbox-sized piece of cheese, otherwise the fat content of the dish will be much higher. Even lean mince and lower fat cheese contain appreciable amounts of fat. Using ostrich mince allows you to use double the amount of cheese.

Beef and vegetable stew
Serves 4

5 ml oil*, olive **or** canola (1 t)

500 g beef goulash **or** tenderised steak, fat removed,
   cubed

2 medium onions, peeled and cut into eighths

2 cloves garlic, crushed

125 ml red wine (½ c)

4 medium carrots, sliced lengthwise and then quartered

5 ml dried oregano (1 t)

1 sprig fresh rosemary (8 cm), leaves chopped

60 ml split lentils* (¼ c)

5–10 ml beef stock powder* (1–2 t), dissolved in
   250 ml boiling water (1 c)

125 ml brown rice* (½ c)

6 baby potatoes, quartered

1 tin tomato paste (65 g)

15 ml chutney (1 T), optional

Nutrients per serving
GI low (43) • Carbohydrates 38 g • Protein 34 g
Fat 12 g • Saturated fat 4 g • Fibre 8 g
kJ 1 867 • GL 16
One serving is equivalent to: 1½ starch + 4 protein
+ 2 vegetables

1. Heat the oil in a large saucepan and stir-fry the meat on high heat until browned. Remove from the saucepan and set aside.
2. Reduce the heat slightly and gently fry the onions and garlic, using the same saucepan and no extra fat. Cook for about 5 minutes, stirring occasionally.
3. Add the wine, carrots, oregano, rosemary, lentils and prepared stock, and cook covered for 10 minutes on low heat.
4. Meanwhile, cook the rice in lightly salted water in another saucepan until just tender.
5. Add the cooked meat, raw potatoes, tomato paste, chutney and about 125 ml (½ c) of water to the vegetable mixture, and cook covered for 45 minutes or until the meat and vegetables are soft. Stir occasionally and add more water, if necessary, to make enough gravy.
6. Add freshly ground black pepper to taste and serve with the rice and a large mixed salad.

Dieticians' notes
• Half a cup of any lower GI starch can be used, such as lower GI rice, pearled wheat or barley. Note the small amount of rice for four servings, as the stew already contains potatoes, lentils and wine.
• Split lentils are an ideal thickener for stews, casseroles and curries, instead of high GI cornflour, flour and gravy powders.

* See page 122 for the recommended product list.

Gammon steaks with apple and cider

Serves 4

185 ml lower GI rice* (¾ c)

4 gammon **or** Kassler chops **or** steak, all fat removed (400 g)

2 leeks, sliced **or** 1 large onion, peeled, halved and sliced

5 ml vegetable stock powder*, sodium reduced (1 t), dissolved in 150 ml boiling water (⅗ c)

10 ml honey and mustard dressing (2 t), optional

5 ml French mustard (1 t)

5 ml wholegrain mustard (1 t)

150 ml dry **or** lite cider (⅗ c)

1 tin pie apples*, chopped if desired (410 g)

60 ml fat-reduced cream* (4 T)

Nutrients per serving
GI low (42) • Carbohydrates 37 g • Protein 23 g
Fat 11 g • Saturated fat 2.3 g • Fibre 3 g
kJ 1 489 • GL 16
One serving is equivalent to: 1½ starch + 3 protein + 1 fruit

1. Cook the rice in boiling water until just tender. Do not add salt.
2. Spray a large non-stick frying pan with non-stick cooking spray and heat until hot.
3. Add the gammon or Kassler and fry on high until browned on both sides. Set aside.
4. Add the leeks (or onion) to the pan without adding fat and stir-fry until golden.
5. Prepare the stock in a cup.
6. In a separate cup, mix the dressing and mustards and add a little of the prepared stock.
7. Add the mustard mixture, the rest of the stock and the cider to the pan and bring to the boil.
8. Return the meat to the pan, cover and simmer for about 5 minutes.
9. Add the apples and cook for another 5 minutes, uncovered.
10. Remove the meat and keep warm.
11. Add the cream to the pan and cook uncovered for 1–2 minutes to make the gravy.
12. Serve the meat, gravy and rice with two or three cooked vegetables or two salads.

Dieticians' notes

• Gammon and Kassler are both high in sodium and therefore the rice should be cooked without salt, and only one teaspoon of sodium-reduced stock powder should be used.
• It is important to use only 60 ml of fat-reduced cream, otherwise the fat content of this dish will be too high. No oil was used to fry the meat – so that cream could be used to optimise the flavour of this dish.

* See page 122 for the recommended product list.

The lowdown on sodium and high blood pressure (hypertension)

Salt is made up of one molecule sodium and one molecule chloride. It is the sodium that attracts water and is therefore inclined to raise blood pressure. For this reason, salt intake needs to be limited by people with high blood pressure.

The ratio of sodium to potassium in the diet is also very important. Most people with high blood pressure consume not only too much sodium, but also too little potassium. Aiming to consume seven to nine servings of vegetables and fruit per day can easily correct a lack of potassium. This also increases the consumption of antioxidants, which are important in the fight against cancer and heart disease. This is a better way to deal with high blood pressure than using potassium-rich salt substitutes.

Increasing the consumption of whole grains instead of refined starches not only lowers the GI of the diet, but also increases potassium intake.

Research has found that if people are given a free hand with the salt shaker at mealtimes, they don't necessarily use more salt when the food has been cooked without salt than when the food has been cooked with salt. So cooking without salt and adding salt at table is a better practice for those with high blood pressure. Also, try to increase the use of herbs and spices, as we do in these recipes.

The consequences of persistent high blood pressure are increased risk for heart failure, kidney failure, diabetes, stroke and heart attacks.

Apart from cutting down sodium and increasing potassium intake, the following also need to be considered to lower high blood pressure: losing weight, reducing fat intake (especially trans and saturated fat), controlling alcohol consumption, increasing exercise, and increasing vitamin C and lycopene intake, both found in tomatoes.

Puddings and desserts

Baked custard
Serves 8

250 ml skimmed milk* (1 c)
380 ml low fat evaporated milk* (1 tin)
200 ml apple juice* (⅘ c)
45 ml cornstarch (3 T) (Maizena)
4 extra large eggs
5 ml vanilla essence (1 t)
60 ml sugar (4 T)
pinch of ground nutmeg

Nutrients per serving
GI low (49) • Carbohydrates 18 g • Protein 8 g
Fat 5 g • Saturated fat 2 g • Fibre negligible
kJ 618 • GL 9
One serving is equivalent to: ½ fruit / starch
+ 1 low fat dairy

1. Preheat the oven to 160° C.
2. Place the skimmed and evaporated milk in a saucepan and stir over low heat for 2 minutes, or until warmed through.
3. Pour the apple juice into a cup and mix with the custard powder until smooth.
4. Stir into the warmed milk in the saucepan and continue to stir over medium heat for 5 minutes or until it starts to thicken. Remove from the heat and cool slightly.
5. Beat the eggs, vanilla essence and sugar in a glass bowl. Slowly pour into the custard mixture, whisking all the time.
6. Pour into a shallow 1.5 litre oven-proof dish, or eight individual moulds.
7. Sprinkle with nutmeg, and place the dish(es) in a large roasting pan.
8. Pour boiling water into the pan to come halfway up the side of the dish(es).
9. Bake for 35–45 minutes or until set.
10. Serve warm or chilled.

Dieticians' notes
• In order to keep the added sugar to a minimum, we used apple juice to sweeten the baked custard. This also helped to lower the GI.
• Although dairy-based puddings are a healthier choice than baked puddings, they contain almost no fibre, unless fruit (not fruit juice) is used in the pudding. This lack of fibre applies to most puddings.

Spiced poached pears
Serves 5

300 ml rosé wine (1⅕ c)
150 ml apple **or** pear juice* (⅗ c)
4 whole cloves
1 vanilla bean **or** pod
1 cinnamon stick, whole
2 x 5 cm orange rind strips
15 ml syrup, maple **or** regular (1 T)
5 large pears (120 g each)
250 ml low fat yoghurt*, vanilla-flavoured (1 c)

Nutrients per serving
GI low (41) • Carbohydrates 28 g • Protein 3 g
Fat 1.3 g • Saturated fat 0.5 g • Fibre 3 g
kJ 750 • GL 12
One serving is equivalent to: 2 fruit + ½ low fat dairy

1. Place the wine, fruit juice, cloves, vanilla and orange rind in a deep frying pan with a lid. Stir in the syrup.
2. Peel, halve and core the pears. Place into the wine mixture.
3. Bring to the boil, then reduce the heat and simmer for 5–7 minutes, or until the pears are tender. Remove from the heat and cover with the lid.
4. Leave the fruit for 30 minutes to allow the flavours to infuse, then remove the pears with a slotted spoon and place on a serving dish.
5. Return the syrup to the boil for 6–8 minutes, or until reduced by half (about 250 ml or 1 c).
6. Strain the syrup over the pears.
7. Serve warm or chilled with 50 ml (just over 2 T) yoghurt.

Dieticians' notes
• Low fat, vanilla-flavoured yoghurt is an ideal substitute for cream on pudding. Not only is it much lower in fat, but one serving of 50 ml (just over 2 T) also has a GL of only 2 and is equally delicious.
• Fruit-based puddings always have a lower GI and GL, and are usually lower in fat and higher in fibre than most other puddings.
• It is important to keep the GL of desserts at around 10, as desserts are usually eaten as part of a main meal, which may already have a GL of around 20. The recommended GL for main meals should be between 20 and 30.

* See page 122 for the recommended product list.

Chocberry pudding
Serves 10

500 g fresh strawberries (2 punnets)
10 ml soft brown sugar (2 t)
60 ml boiling water (¼ c)
5 ml vanilla essence (1 t)
90 ml soft margarine*, lite (6 T)
100 ml sugar (⅖ c)
125 ml self-raising flour (½ c)
60 ml cocoa (4 T)
10 ml baking powder (2 t)
2.5 ml salt (½ t)
60 ml oat bran* (¼ c)
1 egg
1 egg white
60 ml skimmed milk* (¼ c)

Nutrients per serving
GI intermediate (61) • Carbohydrates 19 g
Protein 3 g • Fat 6 g • Saturated fat 1.4 g
Fibre 2 g • kJ 594 • GL 11
One serving is equivalent to: 1½ starch + 1 fat

1. Preheat the oven to 180° C.
2. Wash and quarter one of the punnets of strawberries and place them in a saucepan on low heat. Add the brown sugar, water and vanilla essence and simmer gently while making the sponge mixture.
3. Cream the margarine and sugar.
4. Sift the flour, cocoa, baking powder and salt into a separate bowl. Add the oat bran and lift up a few times with a spoon to incorporate air.
5. Add the egg and egg white to the margarine and sugar mixture one by one, alternating with one or two tablespoons of the dry ingredients. Use an electric beater to ensure good blending.
6. Fold the rest of the dry ingredients, and the strawberry mixture and milk, into the batter.
7. Lightly grease a 200 x 70 mm baking dish, using non-stick cooking spray, and spoon the strawberries and the batter into the baking dish.
8. Place in the oven and bake for 25–30 minutes until done.
9. When ready to serve, decorate with the remaining punnet of fresh strawberries.

Dieticians' notes

- Although this pudding contains two punnets of strawberries, there is not enough of the fruit to make up even half a fruit portion per serving. This is because all berries are very low in carbohydrate. In addition, all berries also have a low GI. As a result of these two factors, they also have a very low GL. One whole cup of chopped strawberries is equivalent to only one portion of fruit with a GL of 6. Compare this to an average-sized mango, which is equivalent to three portions of fruit and has a GL of 24!
- Strawberries and chocolate go well together. Remember this, as substituting half the chocolate with strawberries is a good way to reduce your chocolate intake, which is high in total and saturated fats.
- Although this pudding contains fruit and we have replaced some of the flour with oat bran, the GI is still not low.
- Remember to compensate for the starch and fat in puddings by omitting these at the meal with which you have the pudding, or leave out your next in-between snack. Alternatively, you can wait for an hour or two before having the pudding. In this way, you also end up eating less at your next meal.
- Low GL fruit (berries) and vegetables (lettuce, tomatoes, cabbage, cucumber, etc.) can be eaten in large quantities, as even large volumes contain very little carbohydrate. This helps to increase satiety by giving the impression of eating a lot, and can be used to replace some of the concentrated starch, fat and protein in most meals.
- Cocoa, which is found in higher quantities in dark chocolate, is a rich source of the group of antioxidants known as *flavonoids*. Regular consumption of cocoa powder, rather than too much chocolate, helps to control blood pressure, reduces blood clotting and is good for heart health in general. Remember that chocolate contains appreciable amounts of fat and should be eaten only in controlled portions.

* See page 122 for the recommended product list.

Lemon delicious
Serves 6

100 ml low fat smooth cottage cheese* (½ x 200 g tub)
60 ml sugar (4 T)
2 eggs, separated
60 ml flour (4 T)
5 ml lemon rind, finely grated (1 t)
60 ml lemon juice (¼ c)
200 ml skimmed milk* (⅘ c)
5 ml icing sugar (1 t), for dusting
lemon or lime slices to garnish

Nutrients per serving
GI intermediate (57) • Carbohydrates 15 g
Protein 6 g • Fat 3 g • Saturated fat 1 g
Fibre negligible • kJ 439 • GL 8
One serving is equivalent to: 1 starch + ½ fat

1. Preheat the oven to 180° C.
2. In a large bowl combine the cottage cheese, sugar and egg yolks.
3. Stir in the flour and lemon rind, and then gradually stir in the lemon juice and milk, until just smooth. Do not over-mix.
4. Beat the egg whites with a clean electric beater in a clean, dry bowl until soft peaks form. Using a large metal spoon, gently fold the egg whites into the lemon mixture. Spoon into six 250 ml (1 c) ovenproof dishes.
5. Place the dishes in a large roasting tin. Pour in enough hot water to come halfway up the sides of the dishes, and bake for 30 minutes or until set in the centre.
6. Dust with icing sugar, garnish with a slice of lemon or lime, and serve warm.

Dieticians' notes
- Remember to omit the starch from the meal at which you are also having pudding.
- Most desserts contain concentrated carbohydrates (in the form of sugar and / or flour) and fat. For this reason, they should only be eaten occasionally, and with the meal's starch replaced.
- Dishes with added acids, such as lemon juice or vinegar, will have a lower GI, as acids slow digestion.

Mocha mousse
Serves 8

15 ml instant coffee (1 T)
10 ml cocoa powder (2 t)
15 ml gelatine powder (1 T)
125 ml boiling water (½ c)
200 – 250 g low fat smooth cottage cheese* (1 tub)
125 ml sugar (½ c)
1 tin low fat evaporated milk*, well chilled (380 g)
10 ml cocoa powder (2 t), for dusting
250 g raspberries **or** strawberries (1 punnet), optional

Nutrients per serving
GI low (52) • Carbohydrates 19 g • Protein 9 g
Fat 3 g • Saturated fat 2 g • Fibre negligible
kJ 583 • GL 10
One serving is equivalent to: 1 starch + ½ low fat dairy

1. Mix the coffee, cocoa, gelatine and water in a heat-proof bowl. Place the bowl in a saucepan of very hot water, and stir until the gelatine has dissolved and the mixture is smooth. Alternatively, heat in the microwave on high for 1 minute and 20 seconds. Cool slightly.
2. Beat the cottage cheese and sugar together with an electric beater for 2 minutes, or until the sugar dissolves. Gradually beat in the coffee and gelatine mixture.
3. Place the evaporated milk in a separate bowl and beat with the electric beater on high speed until the mixture is frothy and holds its shape. Beat the cottage cheese and mocha mixture gradually into the evaporated froth, until well combined.
4. Pour into eight champagne or large wine glasses and refrigerate for 3–4 hours or until set. Dust with cocoa and serve with raspberries or strawberries, if desired.

Dieticians' notes
- This is a delicious light pudding, low in fat and kilojoules to complement those meals that contain one or less starch portions.
- This pudding is truly a low fat pudding by definition – containing 3 g of fat per 100 g. However, just over half of the fat is in fact saturated, but at such a low concentration this is acceptable. Higher saturated fat content is always the case in dairy-based recipes.

* See page 122 for the recommended product list.

Tiramisu

Serves 10

You may be surprised how delicious this adapted tiramisu is!

3 extra large eggs

5 ml vanilla essence (1 t)

60 ml sugar (4 T)

125 ml self-raising flour (½ c), **or** 125 ml cake flour (½ c)
   plus 5 ml (1 t) baking powder

7.5 ml gelatine (1½ t)

30 ml boiling water (2 T)

30 ml instant coffee powder (2 T)

30 ml boiling water (2 T)

80 ml skimmed milk* (⅓ c)

60 ml whisky **or** brandy (4 T), optional

350 g low fat smooth plain cottage cheese* (1½ tubs)

75 ml skimmed milk (5 T)

60 ml sugar (4 T)

5 ml vanilla essence (1 t)

10 ml cocoa powder (2 t)

Nutrients per serving

GI intermediate (60) • Carbohydrates 17 g

Protein 8 g • Fat 3.5 g • Saturated fat 1.6 g

Fibre negligible • kJ 620 • GL 10

One serving is equivalent to: 1 starch + ½ low fat dairy

---

1. Preheat the oven to 180° C. Spray a 260 x 160 mm glass baking dish with non-stick cooking spray. This dish will serve as your serving dish as well.
2. Using an electric mixer, beat the eggs and vanilla essence until thick and creamy. Gradually add the sugar, beating until the sugar dissolves, but not for too long.
3. Fold the sifted flour into the egg mixture, but only until just combined, as over-mixing will increase the digestibility and the GI. Spread into the prepared baking dish.
4. Bake for about 20 minutes. Leave to cool in the baking dish.
5. Mix the gelatine into the boiling water in a cup and stir until all the lumps are removed. Cool for 5 minutes.
6. In another cup, dissolve the coffee in the boiling water, add the milk and whisky or brandy. Pour evenly over the cake.
7. Mix the cottage cheese, milk, sugar and vanilla essence until smooth, using an electric mixer. Gradually pour the gelatine into the beaters while blending the cottage cheese mixture. Blend until well combined.
8. Pour the cottage cheese mixture over the cake and coffee mixture.
9. Sift the cocoa over the tiramisu.
10. Refrigerate for 3 hours, before cutting into 10 servings.

Dieticians' notes

- Tiramisu is a very high fat, high GI dessert, as it is traditionally made with high GI finger biscuits and Mascarpone cheese (the *highest* fat cheese around!). In order to control the GI, we had to opt for making our own "finger biscuits", and to lower the fat content we used low fat cottage cheese instead of the mascarpone.
- Apart from drastically lowering the fat, we have more than halved the sugar content of regular tiramisu. To compensate, we have added vanilla essence, as this helps to give a sweeter taste to a pudding without adding extra sugar.
- Since this pudding has a lower GI and GL, it is quite suitable for those with diabetes, despite the sugar in it. Remember that research has shown that if you have no more than 10 g of sugar as part of a balanced meal, it will not adversely affect blood glucose control. Be sure to keep to the recommended serving size and to leave out the starch in the meal at which you serve this pudding. However, those with diabetes should not use sugar in drinks such as tea, coffee and cold drinks that are consumed between meals.

* See page 122 for the recommended product list.

Cakes and biscuits

Gabi's apricot cheesecake
Serves 12

3 sheets phyllo pastry (3 double A4 sheets)
250 ml rooibos tea, hot (1 c)
250 ml soft dried Turkish apricots, roughly chopped
 (1 c or 150 g)
750–800 g low fat smooth cottage cheese*
 (4 x 200 g tubs **or** 3 x 250 g tubs)
3 large eggs, separated
125 ml sugar (½ c)
5 ml vanilla essence (1 t)
15 ml custard powder (1 T)

Nutrients per serving
GI low (10) • Carbohydrates 21 g • Protein 11 g
Fat 4.4 g • Saturated fat 2.3 g • Fibre 1 g
kJ 824 • GL 10
One slice of cheesecake is equivalent to: 1½ starch
+ ⅓ fruit + ½ dairy

1. Preheat the oven to 150° C and spray a large 250 mm diameter spring-form baking pan with non-stick cooking spray.
2. Cut each phyllo pastry sheet in half to make six A4 sheets. Place the sheets into the baking pan, overlapping them to create a ruffled edge effect.
3. Pour the hot rooibos tea over the apricots and leave to stand while preparing the filling.
4. Mix the cottage cheese in a bowl with the egg yolks, sugar and vanilla essence.
5. Sift the custard powder evenly over the filling mixture and fold in, using a plastic spatula.
6. Strain the tea off the apricots and add the apricots to the cottage cheese filling.
7. In a separate bowl, whisk the egg whites until stiff and then fold into the filling.
8. Pour the filling carefully onto the prepared pastry and bake for 1 hour and 20 minutes, until set.
9. Switch off the oven and leave the cheesecake in the warm oven for 45 minutes to prevent it from collapsing and wrinkling.
10. Cool the cheesecake completely in the baking pan, before sliding it carefully onto a serving platter. Use a spatula to do this. Cut into 12 slices.

The soft, tart apricots give this cheesecake a delicious sour tanq,

Dieticians' notes
• Phyllo pastry is a convenient, quick and easy, fat free pastry even though it has a high GI. Using predominantly lower GI ingredients in a recipe easily offsets the high GI of the phyllo. Usually 10 sheets of phyllo would be used as a base for a cheesecake. By minimising the high GI pastry, as we have done in this recipe, it becomes an acceptable, convenient alternative.
• The predominant fat in most animal products, including dairy products, is saturated. Even though we used low fat cottage cheese in this recipe, just over half of the fat in the cheesecake is saturated. This is quite acceptable, as the total fat content is so low, and for this reason we usually recommend low fat or fat free dairy products. In this recipe the low fat cottage cheese gives a superior texture to the cheesecake, only adding an extra 1.5 g of fat per slice.

* See page 122 for the recommended product list.

An update on eggs
Contrary to popular belief, eggs are in fact a source of good quality protein. Even though they are high in cholesterol, one third of the fat in eggs is in the beneficial mono-unsaturated form. As your body can manufacture cholesterol from saturated fats, and eggs contain less saturated fat than mono-unsaturated fatty acids (MUFAs), it is equally important to limit your intake of saturated fat (and cholesterol). There is thus no reason to exclude eggs from the diet – even for those with high cholesterol.

Muesli biscuits with Nutella
Makes 30 biscuits

45 ml butter (3 T)

150 ml soft brown sugar (⅗ c)

1 egg

2.5 ml salt (½ t)

2.5 ml vanilla essence (½ t), optional

90 ml cake flour (6 T)

30 ml oat bran* (2 T)

60 ml digestive bran (4 T)

125 ml high fibre bran cereal* (½ c), crushed after measuring

125 ml lower GI oats* (½ c)

45 ml Nutella (hazelnut spread, available at most supermarkets) (3 T)

Nutrients per biscuit

GI intermediate (57) • Carbohydrates 8 g

Protein 1 g • Fat 2 g • Saturated fat 1 g

Fibre 1 g • kJ 225 • GL 4

One biscuit is equivalent to: ½ starch + ½ fat

1. Preheat the oven to 180° C.
2. Lightly grease a large non-stick baking pan with non-stick cooking spray.
3. In a saucepan, melt the butter and add the sugar. Stir over low heat until the sugar is dissolved, and remove from the stove.
4. Beat the egg and add to the butter and sugar mixture, together with the salt.
5. Add the vanilla essence and mix.
6. In a separate bowl, mix the flour, oat bran, digestive bran, cereal and oats together, and add to the butter mixture in the saucepan. Mix well.
7. Spoon a teaspoon of the batter at a time onto the baking tray, 5 cm apart, to make 30 biscuits. No need to flatten the biscuits as they flatten out during baking.
8. Place in the preheated oven and bake for 10 minutes.
9. Remove the pan from the oven and spread a knife-tip of Nutella onto each biscuit while they are still hot
10. Cool the biscuits on the pan for 10 minutes before removing and placing on a cooling rack.

Dieticians' note
We have used butter, a source of saturated fat, in this recipe for flavour, as a little saturated fat is perfectly acceptable. Remember though, that plant fats should be used in preference to butter most of the time. These biscuits also contain an equal amount of mono-unsaturated fatty acids (MUFAs), contributed predominantly by the Nutella and the rest from the butter.

* See page 122 for the recommended product list.

The low down on snacking

The ideal snack is a piece of fresh fruit – beautifully packaged and ready to eat. Should you prefer a starch-based snack, such as biscuits, rusks, muffins, etc., you will need to compensate for this starch serving at your previous or next meal. This is easily done by simply replacing one of your starch portions at the meal with a fruit or extra vegetables. In this way you will ensure that the kilograms will not creep up on you over the years.

Remember that the most important thing about snacks is that they are just that – a snack, and not a meal. Ideally, a snack should contain no more than 500 kJ and have a GL of around 10.

It is not a given that everyone with diabetes needs in-between meal snacks. It all depends on the type and amount of insulin used. Since most people with type 2 diabetes are overweight, fruit should be their first choice as an in-between snack.

Only the very active can have both starch and extra fruit at snack- and mealtimes.

Crunchy fruit chocolate squares / fingers

Makes 16 squares / fingers

100 g dark chocolate, broken into pieces (1 regular slab)
100 g plain chocolate, broken into pieces (1 regular slab)
30 ml soft margarine*, lite (2 T)
500 ml All Bran Honey Nut Crunch **or** plain All Bran
    Flakes (2 c)
125 ml sultanas (½ c)
125 ml dried pears, chopped (½ c)

Nutrients per square / finger
GI low (51) • Carbohydrates 18 g • Protein 2 g
Fat 5 g • Saturated fat 2.5 g • Fibre 1 g
kJ 583 • GL 9
One serving is equivalent to: 1 starch + ½ fruit + 1 fat

1. Carefully melt the chocolate with the margarine in a medium glass bowl in the microwave on high for 10 seconds at a time. Alternatively, place the chocolate and margarine in a large glass bowl and place over a pot of simmering water, without the water touching the bowl directly. Be careful not to over-heat and make sure the chocolate is only just melted.
2. Add some hot fat free milk (4 t) if the mixture is too sticky.
3. Place the cereal in a plastic bag and crush with a rolling pin. Pour onto the melted chocolate and margarine mixture.
4. Add the dried fruit and then stir the mixture until well combined.
5. Press into a shallow 200 x 200 mm container that has been sprayed with non-stick cooking spray. Chill for at least 2 hours.
6. Slice into 16 squares (4 x 4) or fingers, using a sharp knife dipped into hot water.

If you prefer, you can use only dark chocolate.

Dieticians' notes
- In this recipe we have "diluted" the chocolate, so that eating one square or finger is equivalent to four blocks of chocolate, yet contains the fat of only two blocks of chocolate, together with some lower GI fruit and cereal.
- Despite the chocolate and the sweetened cereal, the sugar content per square is still within health recommendations of less than 10 g per serving and the GL is also below 10.

Pear and apple envelope

Serves 9

2 sheets phyllo pastry (2 double A4 sheets)
2 large pears, peeled and sliced
2 medium apples, peeled and sliced
lemon juice to cover the fruit
125 g dates, chopped (½ packet)
30 ml brown sugar (2 T)
15 ml soft margarine*, lite (1 T)

Nutrients per serving
GI intermediate (56) • Carbohydrates 21 g
Protein 1 g • Fat 1 g • Saturated fat 0.2 g
Fibre 3 g • kJ 528 • GL 12
One serving (without ice cream or custard) is
equivalent to: 1 fruit + ½ starch

1. Preheat the oven to 200° C.
2. Spray a 200 x 200 mm baking dish with non-stick cooking spray.
3. Fold one of the phyllo sheets to line the bottom of the baking dish.
4. Fill with the pears and apples. Scatter the dates and half of the brown sugar over the fruit. Sprinkle with cinnamon (optional).
5. Place the margarine in a small bowl and microwave on high for 10 seconds, or melt the margarine in a small saucepan on the stove over low heat.
6. Fold the other phyllo sheet into an envelope that fits on top of the fruit.
7. Brush with the melted margarine and sprinkle with the rest of the sugar.
8. Bake for 20–25 minutes until the phyllo is golden brown.
9. Cut the envelope into 9 servings and serve hot with lite ice cream (1 scoop) or custard (30–45 ml or 2–3 T), if desired.

Dieticians' notes
- Phyllo pastry is very low in fat, but has a high GI. This is offset, however, by the low GI pears and apples.
- Although melted margarine is used to glaze the pastry, this fruit pie is still much lower in fat than it would have been had regular flaky or shortcrust pastry been used.
- Note the small amount of sugar used in this recipe. The fruit, especially the dates, give enough sweetness, and the lite ice cream or custard with which it may be served also contributes to the sweetness.

* See page 122 for the recommended product list.

Sweet potato spice cake
Serves 16

250 ml cake flour (1 c)
15 ml baking powder (1 T)
10 ml cinnamon (2 t)
2.5 ml nutmeg (½ t)
5 ml ginger (1 t)
2.5 ml salt (½ t)
250 ml oat bran* (1 c)
60 ml digestive bran (¼ c)
160 ml sugar (⅔ c)
80 ml oil*, canola, macadamia, walnut **or** avocado (⅓ c)
125 ml boiling water (½ c)
3 eggs, separated
375 ml sweet potato, peeled and grated (1½ c) (about
    200 g **or** 1 medium sweet potato)
2 small apples, peeled and grated
20 g pecan nuts **or** walnuts, chopped (10 halves)
5 ml vanilla essence (1 t)

Icing
200–250 g low fat cottage cheese* (1 tub)
45 ml icing sugar (3 T)
5 ml vanilla essence (1 t)
10 g walnuts **or** pecan nuts, chopped (5 halves)

Nutrients per serving (cake with icing)
GI intermediate (58) • Carbohydrates 25 g
Protein 5 g • Fat 8 g • Saturated fat 1.3 g
Fibre 2 g • kJ 830 • GL 15
One slice is equivalent to: 1½ starch + ¼ low fat diary
+ 1½ fat

1. Preheat the oven to 180° C and spray a 230 mm spring pan with non-stick cooking spray.
2. Sift the flour, baking powder, cinnamon, nutmeg, ginger and salt together in a bowl.
3. Add the oat bran and digestive bran and lift up a few times with a spoon to incorporate air.
4. Beat the sugar and oil well, using an electric beater. Add the boiling water and continue beating until all the water is absorbed.
5. Add the egg yolks and beat until well combined.
6. Add the dry ingredients and mix well, using a wooden spoon or a whisk.
7. Add the sweet potato, apple, nuts and vanilla essence, and mix to combine.
8. In a separate bowl, beat the egg whites until stiff, using an electric beater with clean beaters. Fold the stiff egg whites into the batter.
9. Spoon the batter into the lightly greased cake pan.
10. Bake for 40 minutes and allow to cool on a cooling rack before removing the cake from the pan. Place on a serving platter and make the icing.
11. Mix the ingredients for the icing and spread the icing evenly on top of the cake.
12. Decorate with the chopped nuts.
13. Cut into 16 slices.

Dieticians' notes

- This cake is a good example of how apple and sweet potato can be used to lower the GI, as well as to add moisture, so that the oil can be lowered by 50–75%. The original cake contained 375 ml of oil and this cake contains 80 ml. Replacing half of the flour with oat bran also helps to lower the GI.
- Sweet potato, apples and oat bran are all good sources of soluble fibre, which slows down the digestion of starch and binds cholesterol. Who would have thought that a cake could help to lower cholesterol!
- If fat free cottage cheese is used, the fat content per slice will not be significantly lower. However, the low fat cottage cheese tastes a little creamier, so you might as well use it.

* See page 122 for the recommended product list.

An update on nuts and oils

Canola, macadamia, almond, peanut and avocado oil, as well as pecan nuts, macadamias, almonds, cashews, hazelnuts, pistachios and peanuts are all good sources of mono-unsaturated fatty acids (MUFAs). MUFAs improve cellular function and are thus the more beneficial choice of oil and nuts. Canola oil and walnuts are good sources of omega-6 poly-unsaturated fatty acids (PUFAs) and the omega-3 essential fatty acid linoleic acid (LA). However, fish omega-3 sources (EPA and DHA) are superior to those from plant sources.

Mocha squares
Serves 16

375 ml flour (1½ c)
20 ml baking powder (4 t)
2.5 ml salt (½ t)
125 ml oat bran* (½ c)
125 ml soft margarine*, lite (½ c)
135 ml castor sugar (½ c + 2 t)
2 eggs
1 egg white
250 ml pie apples (1 c)
5 ml vanilla essence (1 t)
60 ml skimmed milk* (¼ c)
30 ml instant coffee powder (2 T), dissolved in
    15 ml boiling water (1 T)
80 ml walnuts **or** pecan nuts, chopped (⅓ c or 30 g or
    10 halves)

Icing
5 ml soft margarine*, lite (1 t)
25 ml cocoa powder (5 t)
10 ml instant coffee powder (2 t)
20 ml boiling water (4 t)
15 ml icing sugar (3 t)
30 g white chocolate (⅓ of 100 g slab)

Nutrients per serving
GI intermediate (61) • Carbohydrates 23 g
Protein 4 g • Fat 10 g • Saturated fat 1 g
Fibre 1 g • kJ 814 • GL 14
One square is equivalent to: 1½ starch + 2 fat

1. Preheat the oven to 180° C. Spray a 200 x 200 mm baking dish with non-stick cooking spray.
2. In a bowl sift the flour, baking powder and salt.
3. Add the oat bran and lift up the mixture a few times to incorporate air, using a spoon.
4. In a separate bowl, cream the margarine and castor sugar, using a wooden spoon.
5. Add the eggs and egg white one by one, together with one tablespoon of the dry ingredients each time. Beat for about one minute each time.
6. Place the apples, vanilla, milk and dissolved coffee in a liquidiser and blitz for about 20 seconds until smooth.
7. Add the liquid to the margarine, sugar and egg mixture in three batches, alternating with the dry ingredients. Fold in until well blended.
8. Add the chopped nuts and spoon into the prepared baking dish.
9. Bake in the oven for 30–40 minutes until a skewer inserted into the centre comes out clean.
10. Cool in the baking dish on a wire rack.
11. To make the icing, measure the margarine into a small bowl together with all the ingredients and mix to a smooth icing.
12. Spread the icing evenly over the cake. Cut into 16 squares.
13. Decorate each square with a shaving of white chocolate.

Use good quality coffee powder for a better flavour.

Dieticians' notes
- Remember that over-mixing a batter will increase the digestibility of the starch, which raises the GI.
- Although we substituted only a quarter of the flour with oat bran, we also added a whole cup of apple, which helps to lower the GI of this cake. Remember that oat bran can substitute up to half of the flour in any batter.
- Substituting some of the flour with apple has a triple benefit: it not only lowers the GI, but also enables one to use less margarine or oil in the batter, as well as less sugar.
- This recipe uses the amount of caffeine contained in half a cup of coffee per square. Thus it would be better to drink decaffeinated coffee with this cake, or alternatively use decaffeinated coffee in the recipe.

* See page 122 for the recommended product list.

The low down on caffeine

Caffeine is a stimulant and should be used sparingly, especially by those at increased risk for heart disease, such as anyone with high blood pressure and / or cholesterol. In addition, caffeine elicits a stress response, which in turn raises blood sugar levels and may cause heart palpitations, sleeplessness, irritability and anxiety in people who are more sensitive to caffeine. The recommendation is a maximum of two cups of coffee or four cups of tea per day.

Traditionally, coffee was decaffeinated by a chemical process, but the more modern and healthier way is to use a water process. The better quality coffees are decaffeinated using the water method.

Braai dishes

Catering for a traditional South African braai

Braais and South African sunshine go hand in hand. As this strong tradition is part and parcel of the way we live and celebrate life in South Africa, we thought you would like some tips and hints on how to keep these occasions within the recommendations of your newfound zeal for health.

Delicious food prepared around the fire is a pre-requisite, and providing good nutrition at the same time can be easy if you know how. As the host, you should aim to enable your friends and guests to choose delicious foods that can make up a balanced meal – lots of colourful vegetable options, one or two lower GI starches and lean gourmet protein options. This book contains several recipes that are delicious and nutritious and can be adapted for cooking on an open fire … so everybody can enjoy healthy, tasty braai foods.

It is possible to implement the basic principles of a balanced meal, even at a braai. Healthy braai foods should always contain slower release carbohydrate (lower GI) foods to ensure a steady supply of energy, without spikes in blood glucose levels. Lower GI foods are also much more filling, so you end up eating less of everything. If you add lean protein foods, beneficial fats and lots of vegetables and fruit to the braai menu, you can ensure a steady supply of energy with added health benefits for all your guests.

Suggested foods for a braai menu

Finger snacks
Eat just one or two handfuls of popcorn and then concentrate more on the vegetable crudités with a little dip.
Popcorn, homemade, microwaved from plain popcorn kernels
Vegetable crudités (fingers) with a savoury dip
Savoury dips made with fat free cottage cheese and flavourings
Hummus with added spicy flavours such as Peppadew or lime and coriander
Mushroom paté
Aubergine paté
Tomato terrine, etc.

Vegetables
Choose at least three vegetables and / or salads.
Vegetable finger platter with low fat dips
Vegetable kebabs, roasted or raw
Baby roast vegetables in foil
Roast butternut and herbs in foil
Roast vegetables with rosemary and garlic

Salads
Coleslaw with apple and a low fat mayonnaise dressing
Continental cucumber salad
Tossed salad with a low oil dressing
Carrot and orange / pineapple salad
Broccoli and mushroom salad
Warm tomato salad
Mixed salad with peaches and vinaigrette
Layered salad
Aubergine towers
Tangy tossed salad

Lean protein
Choose a maximum of two half portions. Avoid high fat protein, such as boerewors, ribs, liver, etc.
Chicken with baby roast vegetable kebabs
Grilled chicken pieces, strips or fingers
Grilled ostrich steak
Swellendam fish braai

Whole fish braai-ed in foil with herbs
Pork fillet medallions
Whole beef fillet with horseradish sauce

Starches
Choose only one or two half portions. Avoid high fat starches, such as garlic bread, creamy potato dishes and high GI starches such as bread rolls.
Health bread
Braai toasties
Baby potatoes baked in foil
Sweet potato baked in foil
Fresh sweetcorn baked in foil
Hildegard's potato salad

Drinks
Beware of drinking alcohol and high kilojoule drinks, such as sweet fortified wines and spirit coolers, before eating. If you feel like beer, rather have a beer shandy, using lite beer and diet lemonade.
Home-made iced tea or iced tea lite
Water, still or sparkling
Diluted fruit juice punches
Diet cold drinks

Fruit
Fruit kebabs
Fruit cubes
Fruit slices
Dried fruit mini kebabs
Fruit salad

What to choose when you go to a braai

The problem with a braai is not necessarily the braai itself, but the fact that too wide a variety of concentrated starch and high fat foods is offered. One should make a concerted effort to eat smart and according to one's body's needs and not just according to what is available.

Remember not to go to a braai hungry, as you will end up choosing the wrong foods and eating too much. Make sure that you have eaten your in-between snack of fresh fruit, and take along vegetable crudités and a low fat dip, such as one made from fat free cottage cheese, a little low fat mayonnaise and gherkins or fresh herbs. This can be enjoyed by everyone with drinks before the meat is cooked. Alternatively, you could take home-made low fat popcorn to the braai, to avoid the high fat snacks such as crisps. However, pace yourself so that you don't spoil your appetite for the meal!

When the food is about to be served, take the opportunity to assess all the delicious options available so that you can decide which are irresistible and which ones will make up your balanced meal. At a braai, your food options can easily add up to about eight choices. Six of these should be foods that your body needs and the other two can be your favourite treats, such as an alcoholic drink or a dessert. Fill your plate once to make a balanced meal. This means half of the plate should be filled with colourful vegetables and salads, one quarter braai-ed meat (maximum two types), and one quarter lower GI starch (one of all those on offer, or half portions of two types).

Then walk away from the table of food to enjoy your meal within your circle of friends. In this way, you will not be tempted to overeat and you will eat more consciously. Try to focus more on chatting to your friends than just on eating the food. If you do this, you will automatically stretch your meal over about 20 minutes, which is the time it takes for your brain to realise that your stomach is full. This way you will feel satisfied and not be tempted to have seconds. Remember also to drink enough water to prevent dehydration – one glass of water for every alcoholic drink.

Mealie bake
Serves 12

This dish needs one hour in the oven, so prepare it well in advance.

45 ml margarine*, lite (3 T)
30 ml sugar (2 T)
125 ml self-raising flour (½ c)
pinch of salt
2 eggs
1 tin whole corn, drained (425 g)
1 tin creamed sweetcorn (420 g)

Nutrients per serving
GI intermediate (62) • Carbohydrates 15 g
Protein 3 g • Fat 3 g • Saturated fat 0.7 g
Fibre 2 g • kJ 403 • GL 9
One serving is equivalent to: 1 starch + ½ fat

1. Preheat the oven to 180° C.
2. In a medium bowl, cream the margarine and sugar, using a wooden spoon.
3. Sift the flour and salt on top of the margarine and sugar mixture, but **do not mix**.
4. Add the rest of the ingredients and stir until well combined.
5. Pour into a flat, rectangular ovenproof dish that has been sprayed with non-stick cooking spray, and bake for 45 minutes until set.

Dieticians' notes
• This is a delicious lower GI starch to serve at a braai, instead of higher GI bread rolls or garlic bread.
• It is not so much the sugar but the flour that has the biggest GI raising effect in this recipe. However, you can leave out the sugar should you prefer, as the sweetcorn is already sweet.

Swellendam fish braai
Serves 4

500 g fish, red roman, cob **or** yellowtail, whole and cut in half lengthwise
10 ml fish spice (2 t)
freshly ground black pepper
30 ml butter, melted (2 T)
30 ml apricot jam (2 T)

Nutrients per serving
GI low (53) • Carbohydrates 20 g • Protein 27 g
Fat 8 g • Saturated fat 4 g • Fibre 5 g
kJ 1131 • GL 11
One serving is equivalent to: 1½ starch + 3½ lean protein

1. Make a "dish" to cook the fish in, using aluminium foil, and place the fish in it.
2. Sprinkle the fish with the spice and pepper to taste, place in a portable grill and close. Place the grill onto the braai, so that the fish is exposed to the coals and the foil dish is on top. Braai over the coals for 2–5 minutes.
3. Meanwhile, mix the melted butter and apricot jam.
4. Take the grill off the coals and open up, with the foil at the bottom.
5. Drizzle the butter and apricot sauce over the fish.
6. Return to the coals with the foil dish at the bottom. Grill until the sauce bubbles.
7. Serve with sweet corn on the cob (one per person), covered in foil and cooked in the coals as well, or one serving of Mealie Bake as the starch. Add two or three vegetable salads to make a balanced meal.

If you can find only 1 kg of whole fish, simply double the recipe and serve eight people.

Variation
Use 60 ml (¼ c) low fat mayonnaise and 60 ml (¼ c) chutney instead of butter and apricot jam.

Dieticians' notes
• Traditionally, as South Africans we usually simply braai meat, and chicken every now and then. But braai-ed fish can be just as delicious, so we have included this recipe.
• Although butter is high in saturated fat, we have allowed it in this recipe as the fish is very low in fat and therefore the saturated fat does not comprise more than half of the total fat. However, if you wish, you can use lite soft margarine instead, in which case the fat and saturated fat content of the dish will be lower.

* See page 122 for the recommended product list.

Recommended food and product list

Lower GI and lower fat South African foods and products

Barley
Crossbow pearled barley
Imbo pearled barley
Lion pearled barley
Tiger pearled barley

Condiments
All Gold tomato sauce
Heinz tomato ketchup

Couscous
Couscous made from durum wheat
   – usually imported

Dairy products
Buttermilk
Dairybelle, low fat
Parmalat (Bonnita), low fat

Custard
Ultramel Lite

Fat-reduced cream
Clover pouring cream
Woolworths fat-reduced cream

Ice cream
Dialite
Country Fresh Lite range

Lower fat cheeses
Dairybelle In Shape lower fat Cheddar
   (23% fat)
Delite, Clover (12% fat)
Elite Edam (24.5% fat)
Fairview 40% reduced-fat Camembert
   (15.7% fat)
Lichtenblanc, Clover (12% fat)
Mozzarella (average 22% fat)
Simonsberg Mozzarella (25.6% fat)
Woolworths lower fat Cheddar (22% fat)
Woolworths lower fat Gouda (22% fat)

Low fat or fat free cottage cheeses
NB: Check labels for fat content – should
   be less than 5 g per 100 g
Clover
Dairybelle
In Shape
Lancewood

Parmalat
Pick 'n Pay Choice
Woolworths

Lower fat Feta cheeses
Clover Traditional (28.5% fat)
Pick 'n Pay Choice Danish style (14% fat)
Pick 'n Pay Traditional (22% fat)
Simonsberg (29% fat)
Simonsberg 33% reduced-fat (18.7%
   fat)

Low fat or fat free fruit, vanilla-flavoured
or plain yoghurts
Clover Danone
Dairybelle
Gero
Parmalat
Pick 'n Pay Choice
Spar
Vitalinea
Woolworths

Milks
Low fat milk (2% fat) – all brands
Nestlé Ideal low fat evaporated milk
Skimmed or fat free milk – all brands

Dry beans, peas and lentils –
raw and canned
All brands of dry beans and peas, and all
   varieties
All Gold
Checkers Housebrand
Crossbow
Farmgirl
Gibson
Gold Crest
Gold Dish
Hyperama
Imbo
Koo
Lesmel
Lion
Marina
Mayfair
Pick 'n Pay Choice
Pick 'n Pay No Name brand
Rhodes
Sunkist

Tiger
Woolworths

Lentils
Crossbow split lentils
Crossbow whole lentils
Imbo split lentils
Imbo whole lentils
Lion brown lentils
Lion split lentils
Tiger 4-in-1 soup mix

Flours
Chickpea flour
Digestive bran
Jungle oat bran
Rye flour
Soya flour
Split pea flour (dhal)

Fruit juices
Ceres
Apple
Cloudy apple and pear
Passion Fruit
Pineapple
Secrets of the Valley

Liquifruit
Apple
Mango-Orange
Peach-Orange

High fibre cereals
Bokomo Fibre Plus
Bokomo Bran Flakes
Bokomo Morning Harvest muesli
Fine Form muesli
Kellogg's All-Bran Hi-Fibre
Kellogg's All-Bran Fruitful
Pronutro, whole wheat apple bake
Pronutro, whole wheat original
Spar Bran Flakes

Jams
Fine Form apricot jam
Naturlite jams
Weigh-Less jams

Leaner protein choices

Bacon
Back bacon, fat trimmed off
Leg bacon, fat trimmed off
Like-It-Lean (lower sodium)
Shoulder bacon, fat trimmed off

Cold meats
Danish gammon ham –
  Pick 'n Pay Choice
Picnic ham, tinned – Enterprise
Shaved beef – all brands
Shaved chicken – all brands
Shaved ham – all brands
Shaved turkey – all brands

Minced meat
Extra-lean beef mince
Lean chicken mince
Lean veal mince
Ostrich mince
Topside mince
Venison mince

Omega-3-rich fish
Anchovies
Herring
Kippers
Mackerel fillets
Pilchards – Lucky Star, Glenryck,
  Pick 'n Pay
Salmon – fresh, smoked or canned
Sardines – fresh and canned
Trout – fresh and smoked

Ostrich
Klein Karoo
Woolworths

Soya mince mixes
Imana
VegieMince
Vitamince

Tuna in brine
Gold Crest
John West
Pick 'n Pay
Spar
Woolworths

Lite margarines
Blossom Lite (56% fat)
Canola Lite, Blossom (52% fat)
Flora extra light (35% fat)
Flora light (50% fat)
Nuvo Lite (50% fat)
Ole (50% fat)
Olive light, Flora (50% fat)
Pick 'n Pay Choice Lite (56% fat)
Rama light (50% fat)
Stork medium fat Country Spread
  (50% fat)
Sunshine D Lite (50% fat)

Lower fat coconut milk
Gold Crest Lite
Sunkist Lite
Taste of Thai Lite

Lower fat mayonnaise / salad creams
Crosse & Blackwell mayonnaise light
  (26% fat)
Figure (12% fat)
Flora Yonaise (10% fat)
Hellmann's light (31% fat)
Kraft Miracle Whip light (18% fat)
Kraft real mayonnaise light (34.6% fat)
Nola Lite reduced-oil dressing (7.6% fat)
Nola Slim-a-naise (12% fat)
Pick 'n Pay low oil salad cream (15% fat)
Trim low oil dressing (10.5% fat)
Weigh-Less low oil dressing (10% fat)
Woolworths reduced-oil dressing (12.2%
  fat)

Lower GI breads
Low GI bread
Blue Ribbon low GI brown
Nature's Harvest, soya and linseed
  white bread (Sasko)
Sunbake soya and linseed
Woolworths cholesterol lowering low
  GI soy lin loaf
Woolworths omega-3 low GI
  whole grain loaf

Rye bread
Astoria fruit and honey
Astoria Pumpernickel
Astoria sunflower seed whole grain
Astoria Volkorn

Pumpernickel whole grain
Sourdough
Woolworths fruit and honey whole grain
Woolworths sunflower seed whole grain
Woolworths Volkorn

Seed loaf
Albany low GI brown
Albany Olde Cape homestyle low GI
  brown health
Blue Ribbon brown low GI
Duens Country Collection
Fine Form multigrain brown
Nature's Harvest brown (Sasko)
Sunbake fruit and seed
Sunbake
Woolworths fruit and seed
Woolworths low GI

Pita pockets
Anat
Pick 'n Pay

Lower GI crackers
Provita multigrain
Provita original

Lower GI oats
Bokomo
Jungle oat bran
Pick 'n Pay
Rolled oats
Spar
Woolworths

Lower GI pasta (durum wheat)
Fatti's & Moni's spaghetti and macaroni
Fatti's & Moni's pasta shapes
Fine Form lasagne sheets and tagliatelle
Imported pastas
Pick 'n Pay Choice
Sasko Puccini
Spar imported pastas
Woolworths dry pastas

Lower GI rice
Old Mill Stream brown
Spekko long grain parboiled
Spekko Basmati
Spekko brown
Spekko brown Basmati

RECOMMENDED FOOD AND PRODUCT LIST

Tastic white
Tastic Basmati
Veetee's Basmati

**Lower sodium stock powders
and cubes**
Ina Paarman beef
Ina Paarman chicken
Ina Paarman vegetable
Knorrox 25% less salt – beef and
   chicken

Oils
Almond
Avocado
Canola, B-Well
Canola, Epic
Canolive – all flavours
Macadamia
Olive, extra virgin, cold pressed
Peanut
Red palm (Carotino)
Walnut

Tinned fruit
Naturlite – all varieties

**Wheat rice / pearled wheat
(stampkoring)**
Crossbow
Lion

Index

INDEX